PIECES OF MORRISSEY

MATTHEW JACOBSON

EMPIRE
PUBLICATIONS

First published in 2017

EMPIRE PUBLICATIONS
1 Newton Street, Manchester M1 1HW
© Matthew Jacobson 2017

ISBN: 978-1-909360-46-4

Printed in Great Britain.

CONTENTS

ABOUT THE AUTHOR

MATTHEW JACOBSON is a devoted foot soldier in the MozArmy, that dedicated legion of followers who treat each Morrissey show as a quasi-religious experience. Like most Morrissey fans, Matthew's life was changed for good when he first listened to The Smiths.

A Business Connector - living in Aigburth, Liverpool - not far from the childhood homes of Lennon and McCartney, Matthew looks towards the sky surrounding the Salford Lads Club for inspiration.He has travelled the world to watch his hero and appeared on a BBC feature film regarding Smiths/Morrissey fans (including discussing Moz on the BBC breakfast couch), BBC Manchester Radio and a BBC1 North West feature – for the Peoples' History of Pop.

On each, he expressed his love for Morrissey and his treasured item - Morrissey's shirt. Matthew then received much communication from MozArmy friends and from there – he built this book with cherished "Pieces of Morrissey".

ACKNOWLEDGEMENTS

Thank you for reading Pieces of Morrissey (rashly assuming that you have). My devotional thanks to the people who have stood by me, it hasn't been easy I know. For all, your love is gratefully accepted and returned tenfold:

Mum, Dad, Christine, Bridget, Jimmy, Jonathan, Rosie, Ben, George, Colin, Gill, John, Fred and faithful Tilly and Sam. All Aunties, Uncles, Cousins, Grandparents.

For their love and unlimited levels of patience, Angie, Lilla and the brightest star in the sky xxx

Huge thanks to the Mozarmy; I've met so many - all friends till the end.

Sparkling special thanks to Dickie Felton, Phill Gatenby, Sally Williams, Lisa Redford and Leslie Holmes.

Years of rapturous applause to Ash at Empire Publications. At the helm providing support, advice and belief in the project.

And love peace and harmony to my friends; the bruisers and their treasured families - providing the setlist for life.

Finally, but importantly, PETA and all of those seeking social justice for animals.

INTRODUCTION

Memorabilia: *plural noun sing. memorabile; things serving as a record or reminder of some person or event.*

See Plates 1 & 2

Matthew: This book is an attempt to get to the bottom of what makes memorabilia important and the levels of fandom and obsession towards Morrissey from fellow Moz fans. I find the tales behind memorabilia fascinating. I have spent my years hoping to obtain a piece to treasure. Not the memorabilia of 'some person' or 'any event' but the memorabilia from one person and one person only - Morrissey. A genius and personal hero.

I am fascinated by Morrissey. Fascinated how he interprets and describes everyday life, the life I've lived and continue to live. He provides beauty to the flat or grey aspects of everyday life changing the colour of the sky in my home in Liverpool.

His observations are realistic; from the perilous city streets to a perilous life inside box bedrooms; from relationships to the breakdown of relationships; from the cruelty of eating meat to the cruelty of being born.

Morrissey accurately describes the many feelings we go through; positive, negative, sad or humorous - feelings from the self to the soul. His words hit home with me – it was as if he had watched my every move, listened to my inner frustrations and analysed them before he released them back to me in the form of verse. His lyrics are tender, brutal, humorous and serious. He makes me laugh, cry and think – all at the same time.

Morrissey's lyrics go against the grain, they are not

slaves to the standard pop lyric world. He changed the game. Morrissey formed a new language; he dropped heroic, charming and beautiful autobiographical grenades at the lazy pop world, in the process changing the face of music. He continues to do this today at an age when most music frontmen have left the stage or seem content to cover their early, well known 'hits'.

Nobody will catch him, nobody wants him to be caught. Morrissey is a real person, with a real voice mouthing real words. He does not guess; he is accurate, he comforts, he provides. He is everything I need. Social observations, social commentary and social interrogation cram into songs and interviews; he is like no other.

The lyrics and music are accompanied by artwork and imagery close to Morrissey's heart. His personal obsessions externalised for us to peek at from the patio. The artwork and imagery are such a beautiful addition to the music, lyrics and voice. I have spent hours, years in fact, dissecting and analysing the vinyl sleeves, the singles, the albums and the books. From dusk till dawn. From a teen to the hop, skip, flop, jump of middle age. I have everything: records, videos, cd's, posters, magazines and then bought the clothes, the jewellery, the haircut to match the records, posters and magazines. For me, the imagery wraps up Morrissey's music in a style and a package that I believe is the perfect gift.

Concerts: Those who have attended a Moz concert and joined the MozArmy on tour know it's so much more than a concert. A Morrissey concert is like no other. It is a one to one conversation between you and Morrissey, but with everyone else is listening in. The world outside goes missing but the one to one conversation is about the outside world and what it throws at us; what goes on, what to expect and how to deal with it. Morrissey is communicating 'life' to us, he feels for us, we feel for him.

I adore the concerts and I've seen him all over, from my home city in Liverpool to Birmingham, Blackpool, Blackburn, Chester, Cardiff, Dublin, Edinburgh, Glasgow, London, Manchester, Nottingham, Copenhagen, Paris, London, Los Angeles and Santa Ana, San Jose. And Hull.

The build-up to see Morrissey is a very exciting time. The day just starts off feeling different. You wake feeling fresher. The breakfast you have, for some reason, tastes much nicer, your lunch is much more enjoyable - the pubs seem much prettier. The excitement builds and for once in my life, my heart races. And you feel safe in the knowledge that the night will be brilliant. It is the most important appointment you will ever have. The 50+ gigs are not enough, I want more.

On stage Morrissey's is an athletic performance; it's vibrant, mesmeric, spellbinding, alluring, gripping and captivating. It's a full release of emotions. Morrissey, with power, passion and velocity, externalises his internal feelings. His voice matches every word, every word matches the world. I listen, I use his shoulder; both shoulders. The night is a perfect vision painted before your star struck eyes. It is an evening with wonderful company.

One of many highlights was the tour of 1995 at the Blackpool Empress Ballroom. I observed the clamber to hug Morrissey on stage. Each fan hugging Morrissey took him out of my view and I was rather (in fact very) jealous at this stage. My leg started twitching, it tapped on the floor. And then without any planning whatsoever 'operation stage invasion' was born. I eyed up the route, checked for cover and off I went. I ducked and dived and weaved and joined the rush and a push. And then, shazam, there I was

– on stage. I searched the stage looking for Moz, I saw Boz, I saw Alain, and then – there he was. Standing tall, foot on the amp, facing the crowd singing with his heart opened wide. I ran towards him, I forgot to stop, I hugged him, my face into his chest, my arms around his chest. I kept hold of the great man (probably a little bit too hard – sorry Morrissey). I then raised my head up, slowly, saw his chin, then his cheek, the sideburn and quite possibly the best quiff in history. I had made my own newsreel, but the news channels didn't cover it. I didn't care. I was fulfilled. I have those memories and although disappointed the DVD footage ended up on the cutting room floor - my memories are still played in HD. I can still feel the hug, well I hugged him, he carried on singing and I carried on hugging. I can still see my very own close up of Morrissey and the famous quiff – no doubt he has forgotten me, my hug and the new medical term 'Matt's Morrissey hug face', it's the face of fear and of shock, eyebrows so high they could hit a passing helicopter. Hope I didn't scare you Morrissey – sorry if I did. Trust me 'I didn't sleep for about four years' after that moment – in fact make that six'.

LET'S GET SHIRTY

I've watched Morrissey from the front row, the back row, the third row and even formed my own row - a row for one on my brothers' shoulders. Over the years, I've watched Morrissey launch his shirt to the audience.

The shirt is launched towards the North before curling inside out to head South to the fans below. En route to outstretched arms and fingers. Fans fingers like claws, stretch and fork hoping to attach their finger nails to the button hole - to claim his shirt as their own gift from Morrissey. At every gig, as Morrissey launched the shirt, my eyes have followed the path of the flying shirt, I've jumped, I've leapt, I've dived in and at times, knowing quite well I was nowhere near the landing strip, I've watched as the shirt lands and is torn to shreds, I have watched people tug and push each other and then cut the shirt into a million pieces but each person – so happy, satisfied, misty eyed with their treasure. If I was close to the falling shirt or not, I had to jump for it, I had to look like I wanted it – just in case Morrissey was watching. I would ask myself - will I ever catch the shirt? Would I ever have this memorabilia?

On 10 May 2009. At about ten past ten, I gained some clothing for nothing, but worth everything. My Olympic training for jumping 10ft in the air came in use – for the first and only time. Liverpool Empire was the venue I was on the right side and had front row tickets (thanks for queuing up, Mum).

On comes Morrissey, he was 6ft away, it was immense, he began to sing. I followed his path and I followed his words as they were launched into the theatre. Melodies crashing at my ears to let me know that this is real and not a dream. He cracked and whipped the microphone lead at every opportunity. I wanted to join him on stage, but the orchestra pit was too big to leap – he was so close – but he felt so far away. So I screamed, I yelled, I waved, I pointed. He sung, he posed, he moved – I loved it.

And then, during the wonderful 'Let Me Kiss You', he ripped open the shirt and the eyeball game started again.

Where would he throw the shirt, North, South, East, West, no one had a clue. Maybe, to be cheeky, he'd throw it straight down the orchestra pit. I watched his circling arm, and then I watched his eyes, he tricked and teased the crowd and then 'ground control, we have lift off'. The shirt was launched, he threw it North - up up, up and away, it had clearance from air traffic control, I looked at it, it looked at me. It lit up the concert hall, I heard the air raid sirens in my head – the Blue shirt missile was on its way. And then the shirt travelled South again, it appeared to be coming my way, it was! I had to time my leap. I had to grab the prize. In a split second, I caught the arm of the shirt and when I looked down, I hadn't just caught the arm of the shirt - I had caught the whole shirt!

I gathered up the shirt in a ball and in a split second, the shirt was in a ball and underneath my own shirt – yes my very own instant shirt pot belly. Fans clapped and cheered, my reward was here. I was determined for it to remain safe, so it had to go elsewhere – I decided to keep mine hidden. I shoved it down my trousers. I then spent the gig in disbelief because Morrissey's shirt was in my possession – down the front of my trousers. The 10ft Olympic leap had paid off, my inclusion to the leaping squad was justified, I'd made the grade, I'd made my dream come true, I was on the winner's podium. I was the winner, the very first podium winner with a shirt down his trousers.

I left a split second before the concert ended, I ran and I ran. I bumped into my friend Andy, who asked, "Was it you? Did I see you jump to catch the shirt?"

"Yes," I answered, "it's in my trousers!" Worryingly for Andy, I didn't say much more, other than, "it's in my trousers!". I said "Goodbye" and ran again. Hope I wasn't rude Andy, but I know he understands what the shirt means to me - what Morrissey means to me.

Goodness knows what I looked like running down the streets into the darkness of the night. I can't run in the day never mind at night – especially with a shirt down my trousers. I ran into a bar off the beaten track, I was out of breath and dishevelled. I walked calmly to the bar, on a high, nervous and excited. I ordered a drink, for the first time and last time with someone else's shirt stuffed down the front of my trousers. I walked over to a table in the corner, it was dark with just a candle flickering to brighten the alcove – this was a moment in history. I had Superman's cape. And in this dim lit bar, I was about to take something out of my trousers – and so I did, with two hands.

And there it was. Morrissey's shirt was in front of me. 30 minutes ago, he was singing the songs that I love, that I adore, that I cherish – in this shirt. I felt a bit faint. I sat back and glared at the shirt for about an hour, ordered another drink from my seat – well I wasn't moving anywhere with it! I then decided to text pretty much everyone I know and let them know.

'I have Morrissey's shirt'

I'm unsure if the bloke I played football with 5 years ago wanted to know but he was part of my contact list, and I don't think my bank's customer service team wanted to know but they were part of the contact list. My Mum is on the contact list – but she hasn't a mobile, well she has, I mean she hasn't one she switches on, switch it on Mum! This is an emergency!

So, I texted the world, although I didn't realise I had the world's number, they're never in anyway. I phoned my Mum, she phoned my Dad, he was on nights, it made their night, it made my life, it changed my life, it really changed my life.

I have bits of everything Smiths/Morrissey at home. I have ticket stubs, plectrums, T shirts, etched 12 inch records, books, 20 year old NME covers in frames, records in frames and Morrissey glasses – the NHS frames. I even have a poster a security guy handed me at the end of a gig in Copenhagen. He watched me try but fail to climb onto the stage. At the end of the gig, seeing me feeling sorry for myself, he handed me a poster from the side of the stage. I leave gigs with my ticket stub, programmes, T-shirts or a picture with Mozzer's nephew Sam but this – the shirt – this is different, this is the ultimate memorabilia.

On the first night, 'my' Morrissey shirt was placed on a hanger with one arm of the shirt under my pillow – the one that I dream on. Then, the shirt went with me everywhere, wherever I went until no more, I'd showed a few; I'd posed for a few – and then, I decided it stays at home, settled in the one place. The shirt was too risky to lose. That fear kicked in. I wasn't about to let this object of desire loose any longer. I know my luck too well and I was aware that one day I would've lost the shirt of an Ex-Smith as I fainted in W H Smith. So, I cancelled the non-official shirt tour.

WHEN EVERYDAY OBJECTS BECOME PRECIOUS

Now, I have sat and stared at the shirt and asked myself so many questions that turn my memorabilia into confuse'abilia and memorab'ilious – because now (at last) I have special memorabilia of my own. But this world of a memorabilia changes my rational thoughts. It's a world where clothing isn't clothing, where money means nothing and where personal treasures, are personal treasures no more. If I analyse my memorabilia, in a social scientist (or just drunk) type of way – I may have a breakdown and believe me, you could have a breakdown in about three minutes. As follows – be prepared for this…

The shirt I caught in the crowd is a Gucci shirt. I'd never buy a Gucci shirt – I want one – but I can't afford one, so I can't have one. So, fate hands me one, but I'd never wear this one, and even though I won't wear this one. I won't give this one away. It's a Gucci shirt, but sod Gucci, it's Morrissey's shirt, Gucci made it, but he wore it and I call it Morrissey's shirt. And now 'cos I have it, it's called Matthew's Morrissey shirt.

The shirt had a Cathedral-like aroma. So I searched to find out the name of the Cathedral like aroma, was it a Cathedral aroma? But which Cathedral? I don't visit Cathedrals to smell them - so I went back to basics and decided to smell aftershaves and not Cathedrals, I smelt a thousand aftershaves until I found it − I noted the name, the price and then the exit sign. I didn't buy it; I just walked out the shop smiling. I haven't been back in the shop since; then again I hadn't gone in it before.

Last year, I cut a button from the shirt and handed it to my friend Tony who is also a Morrissey fan. It was his birthday present. He was very impressed and moved and he smiled for hours; he secured it safely in his wallet. Today, sorry, unhappy birthday, I wish I hadn't. Nothing against him but, I should've just bought him a new Gucci shirt, not give him part of my Gucci Mozzer shirt, any Gucci shirt but mine. I've hurt the feelings of Morrissey's shirt. More importantly, I'd hurt my own feelings, I miss the button, so does the shirt, it looks sad without it - what if Morrissey didn't want me to do this - to murder his shirt, to de-button it to death.

I have Morrissey's shirt, I want another, but what would I do with two? Would I wear one and frame the other, would I frame both and try for another? What if he asks for it back, would I say I'd lost it − of course not, I'd hand it back and ask him to sign an album cover.

In the years since I caught this dose of shirtitis, I've moved home twice and I have packed the shirt before I packed my own clothes, yet if I'd forgotten or lost my clothes en route to my new destination, I still wouldn't wear this shirt. I want the shirt on display, a display for one, in a frame. And yet I have a thousand personal photos that should be in frames, but they're in an Asda bag. I have no desire to frame the pictures.

The shirt is a constant in my life when the twists, turns, jeans and shirts of life change. "Let life find you" Morrissey says, I will, but my shirt will be waiting with me; well, your shirt Mozzer, the one I have, that was yours, the one I love, did you love it too?

It's Morrissey's shirt and that is the turning point, it's because it's Morrissey's shirt; the singer/songwriter of songs that changed and saved my life that takes it another step and changes for me. The protocol of a simple object – a shirt. Morrissey has now changed pretty much everything for me. From the cradle to the grave, the Morrissey shirt will join my signed T shirt, from the 'Everyday is like Sunday' video and both will remain on tailors dummies proudly at the side of my bed. For me, they stand so tall, so proud, they could easily be an addition to the Liverpool waterfront, squeezed between the Liverbirds, but it's my own landmark, it's my own parade, Google should map it, just keep your fingers off it. The concept of memorabilia drags up many questions, but all I know is; it's my 'Morrissey shirt', then again, he didn't say here you go Matthew it's yours... oh God, here we go again, am I still ill ?

The shirt (not me) was asked to appear on Inside Out and BBC Breakfast. After I showed the shirt to Bill Turnbull and Susanna Reid (who, by the way, questioned the adulation we have for Morrissey, how rude! Only joking, they are very, very sweet, I loved every minute) I was contacted by many fans and their tales of treasure.

There are thousands of pieces of Morrissey scattered across the globe, the prized possessions of the all-powerful MozArmy who follow their hero on tour, wherever he plays. These bits and bobs might not look like much but to their owners they take on huge emotional significance. Here are a few of their stories...

THE PILGRIMS

PORTRAITS OF A HERO

Joe: I've been collecting memorabilia all my life; ranging from old Star Wars toys, records, vintage clothing, and movie posters. Having Melrose Street as my backyard, it was hard not to go shopping for vintage records and clothes. It was what I enjoyed most growing up in the 80s here in Los Angeles. From my collection, the records I listened to over and over again were from The Smiths. I couldn't get enough of them. They became part of my life in every way. I grew into adulthood with that haunting voice dancing in my head.

I would never have thought that one day I'd have such a surreal experience as meeting the singer whom I've listened to all my life. To one day have a conversation or share a drink with HIM… it was something I can't even describe in words. In my collection of The Smiths and Morrissey memorabilia, including records, posters, magazine, t-shirts, concert tickets and miscellaneous items, there are a handful of pieces that hold great personal value – not so much for the item itself but the special, once in a lifetime experiences that comes with the unique story of how I acquired it.

TAMBOURINE

This is a very prized item every time I see it. It is a tambourine signed by Moz and all the band. The story is that I took Boz (guitarist) to go shopping for some vintage records at many shops here in town and also to some record conventions. On the way back, we stopped to have lunch somewhere and passed a music shop. I looked up on the wall at the guitars and other musical instruments, and then I saw some tambourines they were selling. I recalled reading or hearing something about Morrissey performing and dancing with the tambourine and then throwing it out to the crowds and there in the madness pit, it gets destroyed and torn to pieces. I asked Boz if he was still using a tambourine on stage anymore? Boz said no, he stopped throwing them out to the crowd, it was too dangerous. As we were just about to leave Boz says to me, buy that one and we will all sign it for you. I was so happy and so I brought it back to the hotel after our day of shopping. As we got to the hotel and walked up the stairs to our room, we were both welcomed by Morrissey on the stairway. He was so curious at the bagfuls of records and goodies that we had in our arms. He asked "what goodies did you find for me?" and Boz replied "oh this and that… and this" as he showed him a few gem pieces, as we all headed for the rooms. By the end of the night everyone kindly took a little time and signed the tambourine for me as we played pool and had a few drinks. I thank you to Boz, Gary, Alain, Spencer and Moz for the most unforgettable time.

MORRISSEY SHOT BOOK
PERSONAL NOTE BY MORRISSEY

Meeting Moz at KROQ radio station for the first time was a great experience. I have seen him a few more times since and talked to him about music, vintage clothing and other stuff. One day, I told him I had done a few paintings and drawings of him, and asked him if it would be possible that he could autograph them for me. It would be some of the drawing that I did for that KROQ contest that I didn't submit. I nervously showed him the few portraits I did and he signed them. Afterward he flipped through my art portfolio seeing the many different portraits I've done in the past of other singers and celebrities as I describe to him what I do as an artist and trying to show my artwork out to the galleries and celebrities, with the story of how I got to meet them.

That was a fantastic day just having that moment with Moz and telling him about my artwork was very dreamlike, like it didn't really happen at all. Looking at the few signed artworks I have its very personal in every way possible, when, where I did them and how I got the great experience to meet Morrissey to talk about my artwork and to have him like my work and comment on it and signed his name on it. It is something way out of this world.

A few days later, they were to leave to continue their tour. I got a small package at the desk of the hotel. As I opened it up with great joy to see it was his new book Morrissey Shots by Linder. And inside the cover was a signed address to me. It was the most simple, fantastic, wonderful thought and I hold it dear to my heart and cherish it. Thank you so much Morrissey.

MOZZER & THE KEEP-SAKE

See Plate 3

Jean-Paul: I'm 24 and from New Hampshire, USA. I've been a devoted Morrissey fan since high school and spent years hoping to see him in concert. I had one missed opportunity and then suffered years of Morrissey consistently skipping the northeast on tour. In October of last year I finally had my opportunity. I caught the tour opener in Boston and was thrilled for my dream to come true. Seeing him live after years of waiting was a profound experience. The show in Portland, Maine was even better and produced a souvenir I will treasure always.

The Portland show was general admission and I was able to manoeuvre my way towards the barrier, centre. Everyone was squished together, sweaty, drunk and in adoration for our hero, who was at times only inches from our reach. The entire time felt like ecstasy. When he threw his shirt into the audience we turned into animals. I wrestled for a piece and won. A perfect square of his orange shirt. I was very emotional, realizing that I got a piece, and thus not only something physical to remember the moment, but something that was his. (He smells fantastic by the way.)

If you've ever wandered into a cathedral or a church that conducts traditional services with incense, and you've inhaled deeply with great pleasure, then this is the fragrance for you.

The show, setlist, sound, ambience and fans were all amazing. I can't believe how close I was to him. The hope of getting to do this again in the future should be enough to keep me going.

TICKETS PLEASE

See Plate 3

Delia: It was in the early 1980's, 1982 to be precise, that I discovered The Smiths, I remember it like it was only yesterday; I was in HMV in Brent Cross, London and they were playing the Hatful of Hollow album, I heard 'Reel Around the Fountain' and from that point on I was hooked, I bought the cassette, and played it to death! I was devastated when they split up, especially after such a short time, and I never got to see them live but I made up for it when I followed Morrissey on his tours whenever I could, I have included in the pictures a framed collection of tickets from some of the venues I went to see him, the most recent was in Manchester last year and it was amazing. I still adore the music and the man himself.

My Morrissey concert ticket collection is priceless to me, having been an avid Morrissey fan since the 80s and a big part of my life. I will never forget the first concert I went to and the impact it had on me. Queuing up at the venue rubbing shoulders with Morrissey lookalikes, his devoted fans of all ages and genders, the atmosphere was second to none, and after the build-up when he came on stage it was electric, song after song of perfection he had the audience in awe.

I will never forget the sheer mass of fans in the mosh pit trying to get on stage for a Morrissey 'hug'; so many made it, some were sadly thrown out by the bouncers and those who made it I envy and will hold that evening in my memory forever...

Paul: I have to tell you about my most treasured possession! When I was about 15 years old I came across an advert in the NME entitled "pop stars addresses" - basically if you sent off a cheque for £5 they'd send you the home address of 4 or 5 of your favourite musicians,... (sounds stalkerish nowadays).

Well, anyway, I sent off my cheque through the post asking only for the great man's address, and a week or so later letter with his address arrived through my letter box.

I then got down to writing him a heartfelt letter about how his music meant so much to me and how it changed my life, also having read an article in the *NME* suggesting he occasionally visited Stamford Bridge to watch Chelsea. I cheekily asked if I could possibly meet him before my team Leicester played there in two months' time! Needless to say this never happened but having forgotten all about my letter imagine to my surprise when a brown cardboard envelope with a strangely written front arrived in the post with a personalised copy of 'Hold On To Your Friends' (*see plate 3*).

When I opened it I originally thought it was from my grandma as she was the only person who actually wrote to me. I saw the cover first and thought 'oh brilliant she's bought me a Moz record', then seeing some writing on the back I muttered 'oh no the silly old sausage has written all over it'.

On closer inspection and seeing the signature at the bottom, I went cold and the hairs on my neck stood on end, I'll never forget that moment for as long as I live and I'll never sell it either.

Patrick: About a gazillion years ago, in my youth, when I lived in Manchester, I wrote a letter to Morrissey. He responded with a postcard, in an envelope, with a quotation from 'How Soon is Now' (*see plate 3*).

When you say it's gonna happen "now"
Well, when exactly do you mean
MORRISSEY

HATS OFF...

Carol-Ann: Someone made me a custom Smiths t-shirt and we got talking about her experiences. She and her boyfriend went to see Morrissey and the boyfriend threw his hat onstage in an impromptu hysterical gesture. Morrissey caught the hat and deftly threw it back, like a frisbee, into the boyfriend's hands. After the show, they cut the hat into loads of little pieces and handed them out to the people around them – it was cut to shreds. But he kept a piece for himself – a piece of his own hat (*see plate 4*).

Helen: I got a scrap of gold shirt at Sheffield City Hall in 1992. I took it into my Sociology A Level exam as a good luck charm and somehow lost the piece of shirt during the exam and failed the exam to boot (I got a U - mostly cos I was doing Sociology at a night class which was on the same night as Wakefield's 10p a pint night... where would you rather have gone at 17!). I also I have a set list signed by Alain Whyte, Boz Boorer, Gary Day and Spencer Cobrin with a little message from Alain Whyte that says "To Helen and Nicola, Thank you, without you we are jobless" which is rather sweet. I got this after the Hartlepool Borough Hall gig in 1999. I also have two 1960s suitcases containing clippings, set lists - all about the great Moz.

Ryan's story: It was in Reno in 2006. A two night show. This place only held 700 people. The best Morrissey show(s) I have been to. Anyway, this guy showed me where his room was in the casino, through this weird service elevator. So the next day, after the shows, I go up there and Morrissey had just left. The maids were cleaning the room and they let me go in. I jumped in the unmade bed and on the night stand is a fortune cookie paper. It says: I'm keeping that for a better time, that's too juicy. Sorry, drink the rest of the wine, sit in his seat at the table, look at the rest of his baked potato, dig through trash, I got notes his manager left him with a phone number. I go to the bathroom and Oh My God Morrissey's shampoo bottle! Some French stuff I have never seen before. One of my favourite days on earth. I have his shampoo bottle and his water bottle and the left over tea bags he did not use. I love my story behind it. I also have his fortune cookie paper. It is amazing. I would love to share. No one else has a story like this.

My wife doesn't get it but she understands. Sometimes I even smell the shampoo to take me back to that day. The fortune cookie says: "Your talents will be rewarded". Isn't that amazing? The notes said: "M tonight's show is sold out. Call me at this number." I've called the number but it's some old lady's residence in Beverly Hills. When I was in the bathroom I picked up his bath towels off the floor, and then is when it hit me "What the hell am I doing? And how far am I trying to take this?" I know it's strange to a non-fan, but I had one of my best days.

Adam: Hi, I thought you might like these couple of pictures, Moz played up here in Inverness June 2011; what an awesome gig, although being at the front all night was pretty exhausting for a 44 year-old man; jumping around, lifting people up onto the stage. After the last song Moz and the band came to the front of the stage and they all took a bow, I saw the keyboard player/guitarist throw something towards the crowd, but it landed between the barrier and the stage where one of the bouncers was standing, whatever it was had landed at the bouncer's foot, leaning over the barrier with mouth wide open shouting at the bouncer to pick it up and give me whatever it was. Which he actually did (nice man).

Realizing it was a guitar pic, I put it into my pocket for safe keeping. After getting outside, which took an age, I went into my pocket and took out the plectrum to look at it, then realizing that there was something written on it 'Viva Morrissey' (*see plate 4)*, I shouted 'yes get in there!' My own piece of Moz history. And he played 'Last of the Famous International Playboys' that night too. I was a happy man that night.

ARTHUR WAITS IN THE SUNSET (MARQUIS)

Arthur: I've been a fan for over 20 years and I have some interesting pieces that I think you'll enjoy. Back in 1990–1992 he used to frequent the Sunset Marquis hotel in Hollywood and a group of us fans would just sit out there waiting for a glimpse or perhaps a picture. One day, he sent his confidante out and gathered a few of our prized items to bring back for Moz's inspection. Turns out he not only signed everything, he wrote a ton of other witty stuff on our memorabilia as well. I got two 12 inch 'Education in Reverse' singles signed but also in addition "May 19th Struggle and Strife in Los Angeles" or something like that. Also, a library book "Far From the Madding Crowd" in which he signed "Morrissey didn't write this." He signed a bunch of other stuff for people as well, all of which I have a photograph of from the day he did it *(see plate 4)*.

I live in Redondo Beach and back in 1990, there was a "Morrissey Look-a-Like" radio promotion by Richard Blade and KROQ at a small dance club there. I heard rumors that Moz was planning on showing up "incognito" since I knew he was in town. Turns out he came and it took about 10 minutes before some people realized it was actually him. Everyone went berserk.

Rocio: And there I was first row of the Morrissey concert in Lima, thanks to the talented social skills of my long time best friend. She had managed to sneak inside the concert venue after convincing the bouncers that she needed to be there while everybody else was outside on the street making a long line. She gave me the instructions over the phone about what to say so I can join her. And there we were after making a privileged line for more than 7hrs under the sun... we were the first ones in!

This was a promising night for both of us; back in the glorious 80's we used to translate The Smiths lyrics into Spanish from a radio recording on a cassette player. To be there, was truly a dream come true. Nevertheless, I will confess that she had a more loyal devotion to Moz than I could ever claim. This was a day she was dying for; it was like she said "her day".

We counted each minute for Moz to make his glamorous appearance... and suddenly there he was; stunning and flawless, like I imagined. The crowd went completely nuts - you must understand Peruvians had waited over 20 years for this day to arrive and we felt the crowd's need to be closer as they pushed us against the metal fence. Until now I cannot express how I felt that moment, it was a magical experience but for my friend it was ten times greater. Each time I looked at her she had tears in her eyes and she didn't mind that the crowd pushed her, remarkable endurance indeed. Some girls were out of breath so they were pulled out of the crowd by their shirts, most of them passed over my head; I was holding on but didn't know how long I'd last.

Then, wearing an electric blue shirt, Morrissey became part of this story. Provocatively he ripped his shirt apart and threw it to the hungry crowd... then at my feet I saw a little shiny "silver" button. I couldn't reach but I saw that the bouncer in front of me lift it up, I opened my hand and he handed it to me. I had Morrissey's button in my hand. Oh god, I couldn't seem to reach my pocket to put it in a safe place! The crowd was pushing and pushing; fighting over this shirt. This happened so fast. The bouncer pulled a heavy girl over me and it was enough; I needed to breathe, I asked to be pulled out leaving my privileged spot. My friend stayed there for the last 20 minutes of the show; I stood from a far-off place and I stared at the button, it was mine. I was happy like a kid at Christmas; I will have a piece of Morrissey forever... When the madness was over, I met my friend and she asked me if I still had the button with me. I said: YES! and she asked me to give it to her, as her right as she was a greater fan than me (don't get me wrong; I love Moz, he is a big influence for me but forgive me for not knowing his favourite brand of cereal). I was speechless, I said to her that it was mine, that it was destiny and luck. I asked her please not to ask me that, she was truly disappointed, her face changed (*see plate 4*).

Over 20 years of friendship, this button (a plain button wrapped in Aluminum Foil, yes folks, Aluminum foil) was the cause of our friendship to end. I was told that I was selfish and that this was the right way to show her my true friendship. I have planned to mail the button to her, but as for the friendship… "I know it's over".

Follow That Bus!

The 2012 tour to the US was about to begin and the first date was in Boston, Massachusetts. I moved to Boston in July and got involved with the wonderful people of the Blue Rose Society that gathers on Twitterdilly to share their love for the Mozziah. My goal for the concert was to bring a blue rose (that I made myself) and hand it to him onstage, which was not possible as the venue didn't allow any flowers in the venue. I tried to sneak through the back door and this guy told me that he would place my blue rose at Mozzer's dressing room… I will never know.

I went to my seat at the Wang Theater in Boston and even if I was alone I had the best time singing my heart out and clapping so hard. He even played "Still Ill" one of my favourite songs. It was a truly memorable night. After the concert I went to the back door and saw Moz leaving the venue on his fancy tour bus.

I took a taxi home with a PETA "Restaurant Guide" that was given to me at the venue. As the taxi was getting closer to my house I noticed a big bus just like Morrissey's outside the venue and immediately asked the driver to follow the bus, a request that was granted after showing the driver cash in my hand, and told him who we were following.

As this bus turned into a well known street, I knew he was going to the Mandarin Oriental hotel right by my house; my heart was pounding, my phone was dead and I had no pen for an autograph! I gave the driver an extra $5 for his pen and a juicy tip then got out of the taxi just at the same time as Morrissey's bus was parking at the hotel main entrance.

I screamed from a short distance: "MORRISSEY!!" both Moz and his manager looked at me and there I was shaking his hand… so amazed – I was next to my idol – Holy Cow!

As I was trying to speak coherently he was signing my PETA "Boston Restaurant Guide"; he asked me where I was from and I told him that I was from Peru and that I loved his concert in Lima. He placed both hands and held his heart and said thank you. Wow, Morrissey was thanking me! As he gave me back the autographed guide I thanked him and said bye to him and jumped so high… passersby were staring at me, but I didn't care. This was one of the best nights of my life.

LOCATION, LOCATION, LOCATION

See Plate 5

Aubrey: I am 41, French and live in Paris. I am divorced and have a daughter who is 14.

All this started back in 1986 when I discovered The Smiths on French radio. Very strange but true; some tracks from the Queen Is Dead were on and I immediately felt in love with the music and the voice.

I made my first trip to Manchester in 1989 and started collecting records and magazines just because I didn't have an access to the slightest items. Things that would be common such as the *NME* and *Melody Maker* were just incredible for me to obtain. But at that time it was just normal, I had most albums already but no singles and not even a single T Shirt!

I had my first adventure with collecting items on my first visit to Los Angeles in 1990 when I could find everything I always wanted: T Shirts, postcards, records, but at that time I didn't have much money!

When I visited Belgium for my second Morrissey Gig in 1991, I found many people that had the same interest as me in Morrissey and The Smiths, so I started buying fanzines before making my own called "Nothing to Declare".

With the fanzines I could grow my collection with cassette tapes and old VHS with Smiths TV appearances and concert stuff. There was a guy in England that specialized in Morrissey and Smiths stuff he made a lot of money from me!

In 1992 I became a hardcore collector, buying records:

here you can see a part of it. I have about 600 Smiths and Morrissey official records (7 inch, promos, maxi, LP, boxes, numerous foreign pressings).

But I was mostly known for being a huge collector of live concerts having lots and lots of Smiths and Moz concerts: about 900 audios and about 200 DVDs. I made a special cover for each one, it takes a long, long time to do this!

Ever since I started seeing Morrissey in concert, I have collected my concert tickets. My first concert was April 29th 1991 Paris Elysée Montmartre and the last one was January 12th 2013 in Atlantic City. All together I've seen 104 concerts in all from Europe to the US and Asia. I haven't done South America and Australia yet but I do collect tour passes, tour announcements and concert posters. I have about 100 of them but I don't have enough room now. So I have Morrissey and Smiths items everywhere…

But I'm also wearing Moz as I was lucky enough to get some shirts during concerts. I have 2 Gucci's, one Dolce Gabanna and one Angelo Galasso

REACH FOR MY HAND

Jane: I'm from Dublin. I first heard The Smiths early last year. I stubbed across 'How Soon is Now?' on YouTube and decided to click on it as I had heard many good things about The Smiths but had yet to tune in. I was hypnotised from that first listen and soon slipped into obsession. I continued to devour every Smiths album and then move onto Morrissey's solo work. I watched and read every single Smiths/Morrissey interview I could find within weeks and memorised lyrics and quotes by heart. I was in love from that first listen and my passion has not since wavered, neither has my new found vegetarianism.

I love The Smiths for many reasons but mostly because of Morrissey. Morrissey's voice and lyrics mean the world to me. His lyrics read like poetry. I never thought it was possible to relate to someone else's words so much. Morrissey's honesty, wit and emotion make him unique and like nothing else out there.

My first Morrissey show was in Dublin's 3 Arena 1st December 2014. I dragged my mum out of bed at 8am and we took a taxi down to the venue where we queued all day in the freezing cold. I couldn't eat a thing all day I was so excited, I just couldn't sit still. We met so many lovely people while queuing. The atmosphere was positively electric. By 4:30pm we were standing in the now lashing rain waiting for the doors to open at 6:30. I waited eagerly, a letter I had written for Morrissey in my hand and that fateful moment when the doors open; I ran. I wasn't supposed to but I couldn't help it. I couldn't believe it. I was on the first row, Morrissey's microphone was right in front of my eyes.

From the moment Morrissey walked on the stage I lost all composure. I cried and cried and cried. Then came one of the greatest moments of my life. During the closing lines of Speedway (the last song before the encore and also one of my top 5 Morrissey songs) he reached down to me as I held out my letter *(see plate 5)*. The barrier was like a vast ocean between us. I stretched further than I ever thought I could and with help from the other Morrissey fans around me I was able to reach and he took my letter in his hand, looking into my eyes and slipping it into his back pocket before walking off stage.

My next reunion with Morrissey would be in Belfast the following March and although both gigs were absolutely spectacular (especially Dublin) neither could beat what happened at Morrissey's "final" UK gig at the Hammersmith Apollo just last month.

I worked all summer to muster the money to pay for my trip to London and with some help from my mum I just about made it. Arriving at the venue that fateful Monday I was greeted by fellow Morrissey fans, many of whom have become close friends. The buzz was great, it's not often I get to talk to other people with the exact same interests and passion. In that all important moment when the doors opened, I could feel my heart beating out of my chest. Once again I found myself front row and centre, thanks to the help of my friends, my poor mum beside me. What I witnessed that night was like no other. Each song was perfection. Once again I could find no composure but I did manage to cry a lot less.

When Morrissey sang the opening lines to 'Will Never Marry' the tears rolled down my face. He met my tears with raised brows and a slight shrug of his shoulders so I had to laugh. Then came 'Everyday is like Sunday'. I had been trying for a handshake for the whole show with no luck but never gave up. And in a moment which still seems completely surreal, Morrissey walked over to me, reached out his hand to mine and looked directly into my eyes.

When his hand met mine, it was an indescribable feeling. Afterwards I found myself on top of the world. Almost literally, I was sitting on the barrier, one leg over ready to jump but contained by my mum's fearful grip. I cried and cried, in shock at what had just happened. But that's not where it ends. Morrissey walks over to me again and I jump over the barrier. He grabs my hand and I am halfway onstage. I feel him pulling me up. I know he really wants me up there with him. My legs flail hopelessly, desperately trying to find away to get up but am yanked away by 2 security guards in the blink of an eye. I shout for Morrissey and he makes a hand gesture as if to say "aw well, we tried our best" and we did. I will always know that he wanted me on that stage with him which is a feeling like no other. I left the venue singing 'Now my heart is full'.

Olivia: In May 2009 I was about to finish university, I had my heart broken for the first time and I knew that I had to move back home. I had kept my heartbreak close to my chest knowing as soon as I told someone how awful I felt, I just wouldn't stop. Fortunately I was about to see my hero Morrissey for the first time. I had grown up listening to The Smiths. Morrissey's words had always expressed how I felt and they still do.

I got on the train from Manchester to Stirling with my mum. She had flown over to see the man himself with me and I knew deep down that this concert was going to be more than "just a concert."

David from the New York Dolls is on the screen. It then goes black and slowly the band walk on stage followed by Morrissey. I begin to cry. I cry because I cannot believe my hero is right before my eyes. I remember that feeling so well and it's a feeling I've had every time I have seen him; this uncontrollable stream of tears that I seem to have only reserved for Morrissey and a few more musicians.

He played 'I'm Okay By Myself' and I felt whatever burden I was carrying had been removed. A few years later 'Alma Matters' and 'Speedway' brought on the same reaction. When you watch your favourite singer stand before you singing the songs that saved your life, you can't help but have this weird emotion take over. It what makes us human.

For me, Morrissey is more than just a singer. His words have been a vital source of comfort for the things I cannot wrap my head around. His words are there when a person can't give you what you need.

Mick: I remember going to Leeds with my Morrissey-obsessed friend to see a gig in 2011. I can't remember much more about Leeds except that it seemed busy and vibrant and had the earthy maelstrom of a Fritz Lang movie. The train journey from Liverpool was uncoordinated, I should have brought some beers for the journey, though I held too much faith in there being a trolley service. There wasn't. The lifts at Manchester Piccadilly platform 13 were out of order so no trolley service there either. Spitting feathers, I was agitated by the shifting landscapes and accents as Liverpool gave way to Manchester then West Yorkshire. Sunshine was replaced by clouds, slate roofs and rain.

I think my friend had seen Morrissey about a million times by this tour. This was my sixth. Though maybe more. I wasn't sure but I had seen him a few times. I always quizzed myself at how, at his gigs, he performed with such fervour and power. Still that singer from The Smiths but replaced by broader shoulders, deeper vocals chords, greyer quiffs. A Mr. Muscle on steroids and stilts. An insipid mantle of a man who held sway with an age-mixed audience.

After escaping the monolithic busyness of Leeds train station, we had checked in and out of our hotel and headed to some of the bars. We could drink but our brains were too racy and alert for the gig that night. We took it easy. We caressed some of the bars near to the Academy where the crowd thickened a little each hour.

At the venue there was a buzz. The young embarking on their first Morrissey journey, while the older generation crackled like radios in wisps of nostalgia. Soon the lights were lowering. When Morrissey came on I stood back, he looked massive. No he was. The spotlight was too thin for this hulk of a Manchester man. He was commanding; rising and lowering those vocal ranges, spinning those microphone wires with roadies following the trail of those shadows. He started off with "I Want the One I Can't Have". The band was solid, Boz Boorer was the anchor to the big boat Morrissey. Jesse Tobias was confident and prudent but careful with the notes. Solomon Walker bristling in the musical spaces. Morrissey was up for this; hearty keen and beautifully huge.

I was happy to watch by a cider bar as androgynous young men sporting skyscraper quiffs jostled before me and young girls giggled and mouthed the words. It was all impressive. Morrissey did a rendition of Lou Reed's "Satellite of Love" a vocal soliloquy of jealous love. I loved the empty loneliness of "I Know It's Over" to the brisk and poppy "Alma Matters" He finished with "First of the Gang to Die" and before a sweating bulge of bodies made it to the door he encored with "Panic". My friend was happy; swooned and swollen with a three course musical meal of Morrissey.

Our adrenalin was still pumping and there was enough time for more drinks. We left the venue and headed away to find a bar that was quiet and out the way. We walked a little while till we spied a narrow walkway into a cobbled courtyard. There were tables and chairs and a few people drinking but not many. It reminded me of a couple of bars and pubs in Liverpool, so I felt a little at home there. It was called A Nation of Shopkeepers. I liked it. It was summer and quite mild so we sat out in the courtyard. First drinks were down to me. The bar was inside and up some steps. And I remembered the venue having a rustic bohemian type feel with simple tables and school desk chairs. The bar was long and had a raised bit you had to climb two steps to get to.

The heat from the gig was evaporating from my body in the summer night now and it was getting colder. I smoked a cigar in the courtyard sipping on gin and tonic.

My friend said he would go the bar. A couple of minutes later, he reappeared, his face beaming like a Christmas tree.

"Come here." he shouted.

I was a bit puzzled. I walked up the steps towards him.

"You won't believe this!" His eyes were spinning like massive saucers. Pupils dilated, there was so much childlike happiness in his face. I was amused but intrigued. "You won't believe this. Boz Boorer and the band are in here!"

I was like "okay" we just left them at a gig and they are here buying drinks. I asked if the main man was there, after all he'd be the only one I would recognize. No sign of him. I walked into the bar now and we were seated away from them but not too far. They would have to pass us to go the toilet anyway. My friend was buzzing, this was surreal. The bar was around the corner from the venue and it was empty and the Morrissey band were all there sitting and chatting. Undisturbed by the hysteria they had just entertained for two hours.

"Oh he was here before," I said indicating one of them, "I saw him at the bar."

It was Boz Boorer. I got served before him. My friend was like "What!" It was funny that I didn't know them. Really. It meant so much to my friend. I was kind of "let's go and chat to them" but my mate was shy. For once he was shy. Stymied by some paralysis. It wasn't like him. He kept looking at them. The guitar player was there; he had long fingers and a long face with a Texan tan. The bass player was there and the drummer too and some woman among the entourage. They chatted among themselves and didn't see us edge closer to their outer circle of closeness. You could probably hear their conversations but the music was quite loud. Again, my friend kept looking at them eyes glazed and infatuated.

"Well are you going over to them?" I asked.

"What?"

"You know, chat with them? Say how you loved the gig? Ask where Morrissey is? Get their autograph?"

"Will you go over?" I was thinking about that but it wouldn't have been the same and besides my friend would have hated that looking back.

"Nah this is your thing, your memories to keep."

What I can recall was that my friend started talking to Jesse Tobias and he sat with us for a bit. He was nice, slender and friendly. I never knew then that he had once been a replacement for Frusciante in the Chilli Peppers and had toured with Alanis Morrisette. They chatted and I was just listening. My mate got his autograph. He asked "where is the big man" Jesse said "He does his own thing."

In my own head I was like well where is he? Is he reading Larkin or watching Corry on catch up? It's funny because performers need to "come down" from a gig. They are hyped up; some take drugs, others hit the booze and I like to think Morrissey would maybe call his mum or watch some TV wearing velvet slippers or listen to New York Dolls. Who knows?

Eventually my friend worked the room and asked for the autographs of all the band. Leaving Boz till the last. The greetings were brief and to the point. But the autographs had been done and he came back and sat with me staring at them.

They stayed there in the bar and we left them deep in conversation. I was happy my friend had been so close to the action. It was a nice thing to happen. Nice in the memory even for me. We stumbled out of that bar guided by a moon and a slither of stars much closer to home.

"Here you go – have these " my friend said and handed me the autographs (*see plate 5*). "Welcome to the MozArmy!" he said.

I smiled and placed the autographs in my pocket.

About five minutes later, he said. "Sorry, I miss the autographs – can I have them back?"

I couldn't say "No" as an outsider - with the outsiders – I returned them to my friend, he looked complete.

Oh MozArmy – so much to answer for… but no one to answer to!

MOZZER'S DAY IN BEATLE WORLD

Pete: It was early morning as I walked past the Liverpool Empire, the doors were opened and something stopped me in my tracks - almost inviting me in. I knew Morrissey was due to play here, but between myself and my friends we hadn't worked out who was going to buy the tickets. So, I stopped and stared, and thought about what to do; I wanted the tickets, but we didn't want too many. This was in the days before mobile phones, so I walked to a phone box and called a couple of friends – no answer. I called again – no answer. And then the phone box chewed up all my change. So, I walked back over and took a punt. At the counter, I heard the kind lady offer kind words "second row ok?", "of course!" I replied. My friends and I had never seen Morrissey, we had adored him from afar but now we wouldn't be too far away. There would be just a front row standing in the way – oh and a 12ft orchestra pit.

On the day of the gig, my friends and I met in Mathew St. Home of the Beatles, but today, it was Morrissey Day. We sat and had drinks in the Beatles stomping ground; The Cavern, the Grapes, the White Star – but, our minds were deep in the Salford Lads club, The Ritz and Strangeways. We had drinks – we had food – we had more drinks…. and then, no more food - just more drinks.

We headed over to the Empire. Throughout the day we had spotted Moz fans, quiffed up, black jeans and DMs – and here I was amongst them, quiffed up, black jeans and DMs.

Fans flocked around the venue. We headed inside, scanned the merchandise and scanned the bar. Quick drink and then we took our seats.

As the lights dimmed, a single green neon light lit up the stage and then the screams increased. And there he was, at first, a silhouette – with a quiff, my friend said – "it's him, I can't believe it's him". The lights shone as the concert began – fans stormed forward, skipping seats and rows, the second row turned into the first row and the third row turned into the second row. Chairs were thrown into the orchestra pit. A fan handed me a chair – Morrissey still singing raised an eyebrow, he saw the frenzy, he felt the frenzy – I felt the weight of a chair as I was asked to drop it into the orchestra pit!

During 'Disappointed' he didn't disappoint. During the line, "there's nowhere to go but down" – he pointed at me, I was standing on a seat, perched on a shoulder – to get down. I smiled and I will always treasure that memory. The end of the gig brought the lights up - and the shirt battle commenced. I tugged and pushed, shoved, grunted and rushed and pushed. I had to be involved. And then a fan handed me a piece of shirt. I was happy and took the shirt outside and split it with my friends. The day was complete, happy in a haze – I headed home, via a bottle of wine back in the Grapes. Well, we had to discuss the show, the setlist, the lights, the chairs, and the merchandise we had bought. It had been Mozzer's day in a Beatles world (*see plate 5*).

FAME FAME FAMOUS WORLD

See plate 6

Morrissey Peepholism

Kieran: I have around 15 books about Morrissey and The Smiths but this is number one by a mile. Visually, just like Morrissey's carefully selected imagery and artwork, it's beautiful. For me, the artwork, posters and T-shirts are really important. For over 30 years, Morrissey has absolutely nailed it. This book covers The Smiths and the early solo years. It is a prized possession.

This was a present for my 30th birthday last year and is signed by the photographer, Paul Spencer. This is my all-time favourite image of Morrissey. It took so long to track down and I wouldn't have been able to do it without the help of a #MozArmy tweet. It has pride of place in my living room.

A collection of my favourite T-shirts

Again, Morrissey has always got his T-shirts spot on. This collection includes his 50th birthday T-shirt, purchased at the Apollo, and two original Smiths T-shirts (Sheila Take a Bow and The Queen Is Dead) purchased for a little more than what I should have paid on e-bay!

The Roundhouse Camden 2008 Poster

I attended this amazing concert on Tuesday 22nd January. It was an incredible concert in which 15 of my friends travelled from the midlands to go to. This poster, which is 1 of the 100 made, I have in my living room and reminds me of one of the best nights watching Morrissey I have ever had. I spoke to Russell Brand twice at this concert and he was very charming.

David Walliams & Louis Theroux

These pictures were taken last month at The Hammersmith Apollo. I am a huge fan of Louis and I was really pleased to see him sat in the row in front of us. He was well into Moz, singing loudly and nodding his head enthusiastically throughout.

After meeting Louis, I noticed David Walliams at the end of the row. I chatted to him for a couple of minutes, he complimented me on my jacket and said that he felt Morrissey was on better form than ever. Meeting two men that I really admire loving my favourite singer made this special night even more special.

A BRUISING TALE

It's time the tale were told,
of how I got a shirt and made me bold…

Lorna: I was at the Morrissey gig on 21st September 2015 at the Hammersmith Apollo. This was announced by Morrissey as likely being his last UK date ever. So when the encore of The Queen Is Dead started to play I got pulled by two young lads into the 'Moz pit'. I'd never been in a Moz pit before so I went for it big time seeing as I thought I'd never see him I'm the UK again.

I was rammed up against bodies but I loved every minute of it. Moz was wearing the fabulous Dries Van Noten shirt that he wore on The Tonight Show singing 'Kiss Me A Lot' – it's my fave shirt of his. It reminds me of a Quality Street wrapper. I soon realised he would be ripping this off and throwing it into the crowd. When it came in my direction I knew I had to grab a piece.

This was a special gig and a special shirt to me. I had seen plenty of others from the MozArmy with a piece but I really wanted a piece of this particular shirt. So it came towards me and I managed to grab on. I am a short girl so I was overwhelmed with the jostling and pulling but I still didn't let go. One man started to assault me and punch me repeatedly on the arm calling me a c★★★ saying I was on top of someone. I had two men on top of me. It was upsetting but I still didn't let go. Eventually security realised my plight and how much I needed a piece of the shirt and he cut me a good sized piece of it and a kind young man helped me on my feet.

I was rather shaken by the whole incident but I got the

prize. I had severe bruising on my arm due to that person hitting me and I broke my finger (It was in a splint and needed surgery) but I got something that means a lot to me. I got THAT shirt and it smelled divine. Morrissey uses a particular scent that smells like church incense.

I also cut some pieces of the shirt and gave it to 3 people and I framed the remainder (*see plate 6*).

I've also made a memory locket from the fabric and it is double sided. A kind friend, Julie Hamill, sent me a piece of the shirt from the Sunday gig of the 20th September. Another reminder of such a wonderful weekend.

I am aware I put myself in a dangerous position and I didn't ask to be assaulted but I feel lucky that I got a piece of shirt from his 'likely' final UK gig. I have a piece of Moz memorabilia that is just special. Lots of people won't understand why I did it but the MozArmy will.

PIECES OF THE EMPIRE

Gary: July 24th 1991 – a date that stirs strong memories. I think it was early June 1991 on a Friday afternoon when I was reading the *Liverpool Echo*, looking at the weekly adverts for upcoming gigs. Nothing exciting to report but then on another page, there was a story. A Morrissey story. Morrissey to play the Liverpool Empire in July! This was a time before the internet had become pretty much the only way to secure tickets. A quick chat with dad ensued about using his credit card and then a phone call to the Empire.

"Hi, I have read in the Echo that Morrissey is playing. When are the tickets on sale?"

The guy down the phone replied, "They haven't gone on sale just yet but they have just arrived in the office. Do you want to buy one?"

Not one ticket had been sold!

"Where would you like to sit?"

"Well, if none have been sold, can I have the middle seat on the front row of the stalls please?"

And that is how it started. My first Morrissey gig. In my hometown. I was a student at the time and had just returned from a year out in France. I returned to the UK safe in the knowledge that I had spread the word of Morrissey as much as I could across France. Morrissey had become an obsession over the previous 4 years. I was 17 when Strangeways came out and I listened to it incessantly. The solo Morrissey saw me take a natural step to Morrissey fandom. I had missed out on the Wolverhampton gig and Morrissey just didn't seem to tour. The 'Kill Uncle' tour was my chance and I now had the first ticket for his Liverpool gig.

Fast forward to that fateful night; a few beers at the (in) famous Penny Farthing pub over the road from the Empire with a couple of mates and then into the beautiful theatre. I took my seat – dead centre, front row. Disappointingly I discovered the orchestra pit meant there was a good 10 foot gulf between me and the stage. Oh and it was about 20 feet deep! I start to take it all in and then I turn to meet my neighbour for the next 2 hours. It's only the lad off the Hulmerist video (DVDs did not exist yet!) – you know the one, the guy who is at the front of the Wolverhampton queue who keeps saying "I can't believe it!". I double check. "Are you the one from the Hulmerist vid…" "Yes," came the quick response. The poor lad was obviously asked this question a lot!

The gig was simply breath-taking. The seats were redundant of course. Fairly quickly a procession of torn up seats came overhead, tossed into the orchestra pit. I got hold of Morrissey's mic stand at one stage but the gaping pit was just too wide to allow any shaking of hands. I have found a recording of the gig online and it still sends shivers down the spine. The encore, however, delivered a surprise. Morrissey had reappeared for 'Disappointed' and he brandished a signed tambourine. I had no idea he was about to launch it into the crowd but as he did I followed the flight and like a cricketer in the slips I flung a hand at it. I caught it! Oh, and another bloke caught it too. The small metallic cymbals dug into my fingers but I was not for letting go! The two of us clung onto the tambourine as if our lives depended on it and Morrissey disappeared for the final time. As the audience departed row after row of broken seats became visible and the two of us were still clinging onto that bloody tambourine. A friend of mine, Greg, came over and politely explained to the other guy that there was no way on earth that I was ever going to let go of that tambourine. His words worked a treat and suddenly I was the only person holding the tambourine. At that moment I then realised it was SIGNED! By MORRISSEY!

I slipped it under my t-shirt and headed towards the stage door. Morrissey had long gone it seemed but my small, circular bump was the centre of attention. Loads of people were asking me, "Was it you who got the tambourine?" I feared it would be snatched as soon as I revealed it but as the crowd grew thinner I relaxed and showed off my prize. I felt like a minor celebrity as people took photos of their mates with me and the tambourine – I wish I could see some of those pictures! On the bus home I just gazed at it and could not believe I had it. My parents were less than impressed as I showed it off to them but for me it was now a treasured possession.

In other Morrissey concerts I got close to a second. Later that year in Kilburn about eight of us grabbed onto the tambourine and we all ended up with tiny splinters of wood and tambourine skin. My first Morrissey concert gave me my most cherished Morrissey memory but each concert is special for different reasons (*see plate 6 & 7*).

Fast forward to 2006 and another Liverpool gig but this time at the Philharmonic Hall. I had a seat in Row G. No orchestra pit at the Phil. The stage is about 4 feet off the floor and there is no gap at all between stage and stalls. Two minutes before the great man enters the stage the bouncers gesture to the front two rows to come towards the stage. "Bugger this!" I thought and I went straight to the front. Once again I was at the front, dead centre. This time there was no distance between us. For the whole gig I was within inches of Morrissey. It is as if he is performing live in my front room. For the whole gig I could reach out and touch him. However, I resist the temptation. I just stand there in awe of a man who is singing his heart out inches away from me. 'Pigsty' that night was breath-taking.

This was probably my best Morrissey gig ever. No tambourine this time but I did get my first ever Morrissey Setlist after years of hanging around after gigs as well as an extremely battered drumstick.

Fellow Morrissey fans will know what all of these things mean.

They mean everything…

NINETEEN EIGHTY-HATE

Angie: I left home at the age of 20 in 1992 to move from my home town Huddersfield to Manchester to complete my degree studies in Salford and Bolton. I was 15 going on 16, it was just after I'd left secondary education in 1988 and I was waiting for my Youth Training Scheme to kick in. I'd heard of The Smiths whilst I was at school as they were very successful in terms of hits, but I didn't think much to them as I had completely the wrong idea. I didn't mind 'Ask' and 'Girlfriend in a Coma',

Suedehead had intrigued me I must admit, but I was completely floored when 'Everyday is Like Sunday' floated so beautifully out of the airwaves. I just could not get that song out of my head, nor did I want to! At that time there was no internet and no MP3s, so I had to listen to it on the radio until I could afford to buy it. I would obsessively switch stations all day so that I could hear it over and over again.

I recall sitting outside my brother's room one Sunday when my radio broke (disaster!) whilst the Top 40 chart rundown was on, and my little sister exclaiming "Oh no, it's that Morrissey, I can't stand him!". I remember saying something like "I know, isn't he awful!" but what I was actually thinking was "Dear God, don't let this song ever end, don't let it stop, I'll just die if it does!".

Once the live album Rank was released, I decided that I had to be brave and buy it as I knew that really, I had no choice in the matter whatsoever. It was destined to be! And I am glad I did. It was the most amazing thing I'd ever heard in my entire life! Rank was actually the first Smiths album I ever bought. Hearing it via my walkman (the music tool of choice, back in the day!) whilst sat at the family dining table was the best thing EVER! I knew then that things were never going to be the same again. It felt great that I had access to another world that my family was not a part of, I don't mean this in a nasty way but it was something that was mine and my parents couldn't do anything about it. An amazing lifetime event which will stay with me forever!

I started on a voracious and urgent mission to purchase all of the albums by The Smiths when I was 16 (on cassette, which I still have now!), I recall being sat in the dark at the bottom of the stairs of the family home on my own as everyone else was out, listening to The Smiths for the first time on my trusty old walkman. Talk about my tiny mind being blown! It was an amazing moment in my life which I have never forgotten and for some reason 'Some Girls are Bigger than Others' made me giggle like mad as I knew it was a bit saucy! Love it! Within a few weeks I'd bought all of the albums by The Smiths, and by the end of Nineteen Eighty Hate I was a fully-fledged fan!

On 'Meat is Murder' it took about a year for me to be able to listen to 'The Headmaster Ritual' without sniggering especially as my primary school days were particularly brutal (I haven't forgotten being caned by my Headmaster because I was late, crime of the bloody century I'm sure!) before Corporal Punishment was thankfully abolished.

When I'd bought The Smiths and Hatful of Hollow (on the same day, from the sadly defunct Big Tree Records in Huddersfield), I recall that I walked to 'work' (my Youth Training Scheme placement at the local council Education Office) in Huddersfield Town Centre and home again along Somerset Road; it was a gorgeous, sunny day and I remember taking in the amazing lyrics and musical genius and being in absolute awe, not to mention realising that I was proper hooked on and smitten with these bright young men from Manchester! Talk about being gutted that I'd not paid more attention to them before they split up! 'Strangeways, Here We Come' was so obviously the last hurrah, a fond farewell, sheer, joyous frippery, and saddest of all, a parting of the ways, but ultimately a fantastic way to end an esteemed "career", if you will.

I saw Morrissey live at the following venues/events; Wembley Arena in July 1991, Hammersmith Odeon in October 1991, Madstock at Finsbury Park in August 1992, The Apollo, Manchester, December 1992, Alexandra

Palace, London, in December 1992, The Astoria Theatre, London, December 1992, St George's Hall, Bradford, February 1995, Brixton Academy, February 1995, Drury Lane Theatre, London, February 1995.

I started collecting Smiths and Morrissey paraphernalia such as vinyl, books, badges etc when I bought 'Rank'. I have a nice collection of cassettes, CDs, vinyl, DVDs, VHS tapes, books, tour programmes, badges, magazines, scrapbooks, clippings, fanzines, postcards, posters, t-shirts and the like. I've started collecting again relatively recently after replacing some CDs lost in a house move some 10 years or so before which fired up my interest again.

I have a tattoo and it says 'Oh Manchester, so much to answer for'. From 'Suffer Little Children' but although the source is incredibly tragic, the particular lyric I chose has come to be synonymous with Manchester in an incredibly positive light and has a special meaning for me as dear Mancunia will be stamped on my heart forever more in terms of all the fabulous and amazing things that have happened to me in this most wondrous of cities.

In Manchester I have visited the following: The Holy Name Church, Albert Finney's Shop, Strangeways Prison, Salford Lads Club, 384 Kings Road, the Iron Bridge, St Mary's Secondary Modern, St Wilfrid's Primary, Southern Cemetery, Platt Fields Park, Palace Theatre, Free Trade Hall, G-Mex and The Ritz.

A MOZ SEASON TICKET

Jamie: Six nights at the same venue! Six nights of Moz in one straight hit! Six nights of him at his very best! I'd been doing 3 or 4 shows per tour for the previous 13 years and I thought the 3 Sundays in a row at the Palladium in 2006 was an extra special run but six nights at The Roundhouse was too good to be true.

As a 'season ticket holder' (*see plate* 7) we got into The Roundhouse early on that cold January evening and got issued with our beautiful purple wristband, a free t-shirt and poster package. I felt like rock 'n' roll royalty, ready to see the messiah (again). The first two nights were amazing, some of the very best shows that I'd ever seen him put on and I wept like a small child during "Stretch Out And Wait". I spent the day walking around like a gurning idiot wearing a short sleeved t-shirt with no coat just so people might see the purple wristband of joy that was attached to my left wrist.

Like so many things in the world of Moz, it didn't all go to plan... The voice faded, lines struck and we could have no more after the very beginning of the 3rd night. I was back in tears again as Brand, Walliams and Ross tried to make light of the desperate situation. It was all over in half the time it was meant to but I'd got the wristband, the sense of joining the hardcore Moz fans. The look of horror in normal folk's eyes when you told them that you were going to see Morrissey on six consecutive nights was something that I loved provoking.

I spent the two spare nights I now had in my less than hectic social calendar scoping out the story that was to eventually, 7 years later, be released as "I Blame Morrissey" so some good came out of the cancellation but to be honest, I would gladly burn every copy of the book and wipe it from the face of the earth if it meant I could go back and have those 3 lost gigs.

Jamie Jones is author of "I Blame Morrissey" and (far more importantly) veteran of 41 Moz gigs.

THE PLEASURE AND PRIVILEGE IS HIS.....

Johnny: Having been introduced to the Smiths and Morrissey, aged 15, in 1984, with the mysticism that surrounded him and a general lack of social media back then meant the only way to find out more about the man and his talent was to extract as much info (whether true or not) from newspaper clippings and magazines – which I still keep; they remain an integral part of my memorabilia.

One of my treasured items is a piece of Morrissey's shirt; this reminds me of a gig at Guild Hall Preston, when I managed to break over the top to get on stage and shake Our Stephen's hand – memorable forever!

From the beginning, this wasn't like other love, it was different because it's ours, but more in a big brother I never had way, offering guidance – when life as a teenager was hard at times. My relationship with The Smiths and Morrissey is still strong and a testament to the magnetic pull his personality has on so many.

My journey into life as a tribute artist wasn't sought but fell upon me by utter chance when I heard a plea from other band members who had tried to recruit a singer with no luck. I had hit my mid-life crisis and thought I could do him proud.

We have always felt if we couldn't do it (or do it justice) then we wouldn't take it on the road, but the last six years we have had – has been a pleasure and a privilege – long may it last!

HE SCRATCHED HIS NAME ON MY ARM WITH A FOUNTAIN PEN

Dickie: I've collected all manner of obscure Morrissey memorabilia over the last quarter of a century; T-shirts, ticket stubs, cardboard displays from windows of long-since-lost record shops. A tiny piece of his shirt is attached to my guitar, posters from tours are framed and hung in my office. The poster I like best was given to me by a worker at the long-since-lost Leeds Town and Country Club following a Morrissey gig in 1999. The image features a boxer and the list of four tour dates. I attended three of the four concerts and I regard them as some of the best nights of my life. Rather extravagantly, I own four Morrissey autographs. Some fans would be thrilled with just the one baby-like-scrawl from the master.

When I first became a Smiths fan in 1988 I did not set out on this signature sortie, it just kind of happened. In 1994 I queued eight hours at Manchester's HMV when Morrissey held a rare signing session. He gladly swept his name in gold marker pen across my copy of Vauxhall and I. Me, too nervous to tell him my name, just pointed at the album where I wanted him to sign.

More than two decades on, that vinyl remains one of my most prized possessions. When I look at it now, I remember my fellow Moz disciples from that day and our camaraderie as we waited and waited and waited for our seconds with Moz. It was also the very first time I'd met Morrissey, so the item has huge sentimental value.

In 2009 I was on a roll and secured two Moz autographs. I bumped into Morrissey outside his concert in Great Yarmouth and he signed my copy of 'The Day I Met

Morrissey' book. Can you imagine the thrill? Morrissey signing a copy of the book that I had written.

Later during that tour I bought a signed copy of 'Years of Refusal'. Moz made around 30 copies available at his merchandise stall. Of all my Morrissey signatures this one is less precious to me as I did nothing to win it. It just involved me handing over £30 in a business transaction.

Anyway, the best autograph of his - by far - is something I will never ever lose. And that's because it's on my arm. I met my hero outside a concert hall in Royal Oak, America. I asked him to sign my arm and I had it tattooed immediately. When my mum saw it she tried to rub it off. It will, of course, never rub off. The word Morrissey etched on mind, body, and soul for eternity.

BEING MORRISSEY

THIS CHARMING TRIBUTE

See plate 7

The next stage of fandom up from attending gigs and collecting memorabillia is surely mimicking your hero(es). Tribute acts are big business, especially as many of the longer standing ones such as The Bootleg Beatles fill a void that hasn't been available for over 50 years.

More up-to-date tribute acts have grown out of a love for certain acts and The Smiths, whose last live performance was in December 1986, have spawned at least half a dozen tribute acts whose aim is to fulfill the lifetime ambition of devotees by recalling the majesty of the band in their pomp.

Of course, taking on the task of reproducing the sound and look of the original takes natural talent, skill and effort so it isn't for everyone. Yet for the participants it has the added bonus of you becoming your heroes, if only for an hour or so…

Matt: So, let us start from before the beginning. What is the name of your band and how did you come to be standing here?

Josh: I am (we are) "Panic", from Dallas, Texas. We were founded in 2012. Panic is the premier tribute to The Smiths and Morrissey in Dallas. We are the children from those ugly new houses and we are available for weddings, divorce parties and civil unions.

M: And you are under the influences of?

J: Our influences include: The Smiths, Morrissey, New York Dolls, Sparks, The Ramones, Jobriath, Oscar Wilde, David Bowie, Patti Smith, T-Rex, Billy Fury, Sandie Shaw and James Dean.

M: Do you or the band have any interests outside of the Panic stage?

J: The Band has many interests but mainly Earl Grey.

M: How did you first stumble across the Smiths and what attracted you to them?

J: I remember it vividly; it was 25 years ago. I was at my friend Joey's house. At the time, I felt smothered and surrounded by crass rock music from Bon Jovi and all those rock groups – you know... well, it's rubbish. That world of music had no identity, they were all the same - it was poor. But on this afternoon, Joey says "you should listen to this ....it's go'ooooood music" and he played a cassette, it was The Smiths and, like many have said, the world changed at that point. Nothing was the same again. I immediately bought Louder Than Bombs – I bought Strangeways and Viva Hate, to be honest – whatever was in the shop, I was ready to buy it. I had to buy it.

M: I feel the lyrics and the voice match perfectly and Morrissey is, I feel, a 'believable' artist. What I mean by this is; he means everything he says, he has experienced the emotions he sings so passionately about. But, many artists seem to guess or live a life in the public glare, miles apart from their words. So you end up feeling they are not so much liars as fake. Their world doesn't match the record. But Morrissey lives a life that is exactly as it is portrayed on record. He lives away from the so called 'glamour of magazines and television' and he exists elsewhere – in another world. Do you agree?

J: Yes, I agree, totally. I also feel, the lyrics were opposite to, well vastly different to, the tedious rock lyrics of "girls, girls girls" and "baby, baby baby I love you, I love you" – here was someone singing Girlfriend in a Coma and discussing on-going fights with record labels. He wanted to sing his words, his way of life and he wanted to sing with honesty and many do not.

M: Could you say he has taken on the pop world and won?

J: Absolutely

M: When did you first see Morrissey live. Did you roar from the stalls?

J: I did, and more! It was November 1992 in Dallas. I bought the programmes and T-shirts and posters and from there on in – every gig I went to I bought the same. I had to build up my collection. I do feel it was more exciting back then, not the concerts, they are always astonishing. I mean the surprise of the setlist; the setlist wasn't on Twitter. Fans stood outside with Fanzines – that was the latest news of a tour, not Facebook. I enjoyed the element of surprise. This year, I was ready for the setlist that I'd read on twitter and low and behold Morrissey sings "I Never Promised you a Rose Garden" - it took me back to the old days. I loved the element of surprise back then as I say, it felt more exciting.

M: You mention buying T shirts for your collection - do you have memorabilia? Does it leave your heart full?

J: Oh yes, very much so – it's everything to me. Everything, as time progresses, it's more important to me now. I have a setlist from a 'Maladjusted' tour and I have a Morrissey shirt. It's in my record room, it sits there, amongst all my treasured items. It's everything to me and more.

M: I have a shirt too – it's a mind-blowing thing to have, he wears it, sings the songs I love from beneath it and the next minute it's in my possession.

J: Yes, the shirt I have is from a gig in Dallas – three years ago. I was with my friend – he caught it, he would do – he's about 7 foot tall. He came in handy! I mean no one is going to ask a guy that big for the shirt!! But we didn't want to risk it, so he shoved it down his trousers for safe keeping. We left the gig early and we ran and he handed it to me. I didn't care where it had been, it was mine now!

M: I think that's the tactic if you catch the shirt, plonk it straight down the trousers! I did the same, it was like having the whole world in my hands (well down my pants!) for once in my life.

J: Ha ha. Yes, I think it's the safest option! I also have a setlist from the 'Maladjusted' tour. I'd followed the tour bus to Kansas and at one point – when we had pulled over, a security guard told me I shouldn't be following the tour bus. I, of course, objected to this as I was a fan – I was going on tour with the tour bus. I wanted to be near the boys.

I wasn't there to cause trouble or be funny with them. I was in my element. I was living the dream. I wanted to be close. I stayed in the same hotel as the band. And on one day, surprisingly, I was in the foyer and Boz came over to me asked me if I knew any record shops? I said "yes". So we all went to the record store! On my return, he said, "thanks for today, in case you don't manage to get anything signed, have this," and it was the setlist! I was amazed, astonished, what a day! Not only that, I got to see and speak to Morrissey, it was the second time I'd met him, the first time he remembered I was a DJ in Texas, and this time I don't think he remembered me. Then again, I didn't give him much of a chance to say anything! But a perfect moment.

M: I've met Boz and the band too, they are lovely people

– I treasure my pics with them too , they seem close and a family – so friendly and charming. How did the records, the memorabilia and the memories of gigs result in your jumping on the stage and singing your life – his life – to Morrissey fans across America? Was it a natural progression?

J: Yes, very much so, it was so natural. Every boy wants to be a rock star and I was no different. I had practised, singing in front of the mirror, dancing in front of the mirror – using a hairbrush for a microphone. And then, my friends are all talented musicians, combine the two and there we have it. The first time was so much fun and it continues to be so. The response is great; fans will climb onstage and really embrace the music and the atmosphere. We have the backdrops, the flowers, the tambourines; the lot. It embraces all Morrissey/Smiths gigs over the years. The music, well - why sing anything else? I love it. I'm honoured to sing his songs. I sing it from the heart. I want to make Morrissey proud. I have another addition to my collection – pics of me singing on stage.

M: I am sure you do make Morrissey proud. I talk about Morrissey to anyone, even at bus stops, and I don't travel on buses! But, I do understand how you have eventually jumped on the stage to sing those wonderful songs. If you ever fly across the pond, the MozArmy will be there. I will be for sure and maybe in Mozzer's shirt! God bless, love, peace and harmony to you and your band. Goodnight and thank you.

MOZ IN THEIR EYES

'These Smiths' are a tribute band from Manchester, who perform the music of The Smiths and Morrissey. The band was formed in 2015, shortly after their lead singer performed as Morrissey on ITV's 'Stars in Their Eyes'.

My name is Jim Thompson. I am a railway signalman from Failsworth, North Manchester. In February 2015, I appeared on ITV's 'Stars In Their Eyes' as my idol, the one and only... Morrissey.

The piece of memorabilia I've chosen to write about doesn't belong to me. In fact, it might not be considered memorabilia at all. But it is something that definitely has a connection between its famous owner and Morrissey. The item is a fax that was received by comedian and long-time Smiths fan, Harry Hill.

One of the main reasons I applied to be on Stars In Their Eyes, was the fact that Harry Hill was hosting. I'm a big fan of Harry's and unlike previous series, I knew that his version of the show wouldn't take itself too seriously. There was also the added element that Harry had appeared as Morrissey too, in a celebrity version of the show in 1999.

The first time I met Harry, I was sat on a giant inflatable sausage. I can't explain why, because... well, I don't really know why. All I'll say is, we were filming a segment for the show. It was utterly surreal but a very enjoyable and funny experience none the less. Sitting there on a giant sausage, with this bloke off the telly, I felt quite nervous and even a bit star struck. However, he was genuinely a really nice bloke, and it wasn't long before we were chatting about The Smiths and Morrissey.

We talked about our favourite Morrissey solo albums

and which gigs we'd been to. Suddenly I wasn't talking to that bloke off the telly anymore, I was talking to another Smiths fan (albeit on top of a giant sausage). We then went on to talk about Harry's appearance on 'Stars In Their Eyes' as Moz. I asked him if he'd ever received any feedback from Morrissey. Harry said that he had faxed Morrissey's people, asking for the great man's blessing. He showed me a picture of the reply. It was an A4 piece of paper with a few paragraphs typed up, but more interestingly, the fax was signed by Morrissey with the message, "Yes, IT'S OK".

This signed fax obviously meant a lot to Harry, and although it was just a scrap of paper, I was fascinated by it (as I'm sure most Morrissey fans would be). Meeting fellow Morrissey fans is always a nice experience, be it somewhere like a gig or at the Star and Garter. This was no exception.

Harry also mentioned that he wasn't too thrilled that Jonathan Ross had played the clip of his appearance to Morrissey, on his Friday night show in 2004. Harry rang Jonathan the day after the show was aired, to sarcastically say, "Yeah, thanks for that mate".

Certainly, Moz has never seen my appearance on Stars In Their Eyes, I'm sure. Nor am I expecting a signed fax anytime soon from the living legend. I did, however, receive a very nice hand written letter from Harry Hill (*see plate* 7), thanking me for appearing on the show and being a good sport. The letter also included the great line "You're definitely the second best Morrissey we've ever had on the show".

HE'S A SMITH, INDEED

See Plate 7

The Smiths Indeed were formed in Liverpool in 2005, after a deceptively placed advertisement...

SINGER NEEDED TO FRONT SMITHS COVER
BAND. MUST BE TALENTED. GIGS WAITING.

It caught the eye of an ambitious aficionado. The band consists of Smiths devotees and outstanding musicians. Their trump card is a singer with uncannily similar vocal stylings to Morrissey's. In a relatively short space of time, The Smiths Indeed have emerged as a fantastic live act, aiming to capture the essence of a mid-1980s Smiths concert. And flailing.

"The Smiths Indeed are a brilliant tribute to The Smiths."
(i-D Magazine)

"An evening of pure nostalgia and skilful reminiscence." (The
Sprout)

"They [...] come closest to recreating the band musically and
vocally." (LA Rock Music Examiner)

They have toured extensively around the United Kingdom, the USA and Europe, playing to full capacity audiences of Smiths fans old and new in – among other places – Newcastle, Manchester, Cardiff, Liverpool, Brighton, Glasgow and Los Angeles. Their first gig in December 2005 was in a small basement bar in Glasgow; the final gig of 2010 saw them triumphantly celebrating the 25th anniversary of Meat Is Murder at Manchester Apollo. The Smiths Indeed offer a fantastic night of nostalgia for those who remember those distant days in the mid-1980s when The Smiths lit up the world of popular music. For those who weren't even born then, or were otherwise engaged, they offer a great opportunity to witness what it might have been like to see The Smiths live. After all, a Smiths Indeed show is meant to be a celebration of The Smiths.

Apportez vos fleurs!

Jurgen: "I first discovered The Smiths in 1991 sitting on a coach on a school trip when a friend passed me the earphones of his Walkman and said 'listen to this'. I was 16. The album was 'Louder Than Bombs'. The song was 'Sweet And Tender Hooligan'. Something about it grabbed me and pulled me in. I could try to explain, but I believe the experience was essentially mystical.

"I'd soon bought 'The World Won't Listen' and other albums – bought, borrowed, copied – soon followed. My favourite song in the world became 'There Is A Light That Never Goes Out' because it seemed to me to be written about me. I sang along to all the songs in my bedroom, 6 floors up on a high rise estate in an Antwerp suburb but never very loudly. I didn't want to be overheard.

"Morrissey released 'Your Arsenal' in 1992 and finally I could actually catch up with events in real time. I saw my first two concerts in December 1992. Another 35 have followed since; each with their own story. In Edinburgh 1995 I hugged Morrissey during the encore, in Battersea '97 I got manhandled by security, in Liverpool '99 I conquered a piece of the West Ham Boys Club t-shirt, in London 2002 I was broke but hitchhiked down from Liverpool with £10 and got in, in Manchester 2004 I was there twice, in Antwerp 2009 an autographed album, in Lokeren 2011 stoned, in Edinburgh 2012 with my son, in Antwerp 2014 front row again.

"I've also been collecting various Smiths and Morrissey paraphernalia. Compared to completists it's not much, but it's still a sizeable collection of vinyl, cd's, cassettes, badges, books, mags, fanzines, posters, postcards etc.

"One of my prize possessions is the tambourine Morrissey threw into the audience at a concert in Leysin in 1991. I wasn't at this concert, but a fellow Smiths fan gave it me, would you believe? He already had a violin from Belfort 1992, so I guess he was happy to share, but still. A true friend.

"Then, in 2005, I replied to an advertisement on a café wall in Liverpool and The Smiths Indeed were born. I had no great ambition to be a tribute band singer, but I knew that my voice was similar to Morrissey's and as a fan I was fascinated to find out what it might have been like to experience a Smiths concert from the stage – the view from the other side of the barrier so to speak. The progression from Moz pit to stage happened quite naturally. It seemed to me to be the ultimate opportunity to get under the skin of my favourite band. Things got slightly out of hand. Perhaps due to how good we were, or more likely due to the enduring appeal of The Smiths.

Over the next 10 years, we became very highly regarded and played hundreds of shows. Shows that stand out include Manchester Apollo, Shepherd's Bush Empire, Newcastle Academy and our North American tour but to single those out is a perhaps unfair to the great nights we had in countless other venues great and small.

Occasionally, as in The Ritz or The Apollo or Preston Guildhall, we have played the same venue that The Smiths or Morrissey have played, and it definitely adds to the atmosphere for me and the audience.

We often meet long term fans or associates of The Smiths with interesting stories of gigs or meetings or even working with The Smiths.

The most curious thing about singing in The Smiths Indeed is that the audience actually responds as if they were at a real Smiths gig. They do the things they did at a real Smiths gig. We have had numerous stage invasions, they want to touch 'Morrissey', they wave flowers, they sing along passionately, they shout requests or banter, they stay behind to grab the set list, they want their pictures taken.

In 2011, we toured North America and in downtown Los Angeles experienced firsthand the phenomenon of the Hispanic fans. Their response to the gig was incredibly wild, and afterwards they wouldn't let us leave until they each had a hug and photo opportunity.

I met Mike Joyce and Andy Rourke in 2005 when they were playing in Vinny Peculiar's band and briefly spoke to them, but I was too shy to mention I'd just joined a Smiths tribute band. Mike signed my Hatful of Hollow cd insert though, and Andy bought me a drink! A few years later, I spoke to Mike Joyce again, over the phone before a Smiths Indeed gig. He wished us luck.

LISA SINGS HER LIFE

See Plate 7

Lisa: Music has been my passion for as long as I can remember. I've always been fascinated with words and loved writing stories as a child. Interested by the craft of song writing, I would avidly listen to the radio and play my favourite music, listening intently to lyrics and the way a song was constructed. My walk to school was when I would religiously listen to music. Having exhausted my ever growing music collection, I began delving into my parents and I'm lucky that they are such huge music lovers and imbued me with an eclectic taste. It was a cold rainy day, I was a daydreamer at school, the music charts were saturated with faceless dance acts and one hit wonders and nothing was inspiring me. Being an obsessed music fan and aspiring singer, I looked without fail for inspiration, something that would really resonate and reflect what I was feeling.

Then, I came across a tape that my dad had left lying around. All it said was 'The Smiths'. Stepping onto the pavement and heading down the all too familiar route, I popped the tape in, pressed play, and from that moment on my life was changed forever. I had never heard anything like it; incredibly incisive lyrics, beautiful and intricate music with an ability to be melancholic, humorous and uplifting, a unique voice that touched me. A whole new world opened up before me, making me realise that being a songwriter and performer was what I really wanted to pursue, I began writing my first songs around the age of 12, started playing piano at a young age before moving on to the guitar. Although my own music is more in the singer/songwriter/folk genre, the way Morrissey expresses real emotions and his love of words and taste in writers and culture has inspired me.

Ever since school The Smiths and Morrissey have been an important soundtrack to my life. I wrote an essay about Morrissey's lyrics at university and so many songs have resonated with me and transported me to special times in my life. 'Suedehead' has always been a favourite, reminding me of my first trip alone to the US to visit friends who were living in San Francisco. They were also huge Morrissey fans and I have fond memories of going along the freeway in the California sunshine singing along to that equally summery guitar riff. I really love Morrissey's solo late '80's/early 90's period, particularly the albums 'Vauxhall and I', 'Your Arsenal' and 'Bona Drag'. Among his b sides are many heartfelt gems like 'I've Changed My Plea to Guilty', 'I'd Love To', 'Jack The Ripper', 'Lost' and 'I Know Very Well How I Got My Name' – I have recorded acoustic versions of the last two.

I've seen Morrissey live a few times but especially treasure the first time seeing him during the 'Vauxhall and I' tour at Brixton Academy. I remember the intensity and amazing energy of a live gig and seeing people in absolute awe of his stage presence. In the heightened excitement of seeing him live, I endured being trampled on by an enormous crowd of ardent fans much bigger than me just to attain a small piece of the shirt that he had thrown into the adoring audience, desperate to have something of his to treasure. I still keep the piece of shirt with the rest of my large Morrissey/Smiths collection which I've amassed over the years.

My favourite memorabilia items include a Morrissey scrapbook from the early 90's which includes some great articles, interviews and posters. I'd save any interviews and articles from publications such as Q, Select, Uncut and NME.

Another treasured item is a shop promo stand from the reissue of 'There's a Light that never goes out' from my local record shop where I would spend many Saturdays rummaging through items looking for Morrissey vinyl, CD's and more. I keep all my items together and they transport me to when I was an aimless young girl looking for a direction and that rainy February school day when I discovered Morrissey's music and my world was changed for the better forever.

PLACES OF PILGRIMAGE

SALFORD LADS CLUB

See Plate 8

One golden stop for the MozArmy is The Salford Lads Club. Feedback confirms that there is a substantial level of love and importance generated towards this building and the sanctuary it brings. Fans always have, and always will, flock to its front door and back to the old house.

The custodians of this building are aware of their part in the Smiths pilgrimage tour and the part it plays in the heart of fans. The media also have a grasp of its meaning to Smithsdom, "Smiths fans have regularly flocked to have their picture taken outside this distinctive Edwardian building and it has become a musical mecca for dedicated fans of the Mancunian band" reported *The Guardian* on 31st December 2007. As such it has become an unlikely hotspot rated the 7th best place for tourists on Tripadvisor.

As a small example, a part of the Lads Club is always with me (inside and out) as I have a piece of the Lads Club in my suit pocket. I picked it up on a visit to the club – it was hanging off an outside brick wall. I rescued it – because The Smiths rescued me.

The club and its local community have now entwined with Smithdom and the club has blossomed into a flowery site of pilgrimage with all the ritual that that word entails.

Opened in 1904 by Robert Baden-Powell (who then went on to start the scouting movement) was an attempt to keep youngsters off the streets and improve the physical well-being of Salford youths. In the preceding 50 years concerns had been raised about the level of gang violence in the city and the formation of youth clubs was an attempt to redirect the energies of local lads into a more productive direction. There had also been complaints from army recruiting officers that the levels of health and well-being among Salford youngsters was woefully inadequate for army service.

Today the club still operates as centre for youngsters in the local community; supported by an influx of willing volunteers – who should be applauded – as they help to keep the area together, by turning the critical cogs of working class society, looking after its people and community.

Today, the club holds gigs, community events and games such as football, snooker and boxing. The club proudly celebrates its history and maintains an historic building typical of a time when Manchester and Salford were the world's first industrial cities. The traditions of Salford remain as the club moves forward.

However the relationship between the club and The Smiths fans was not always full of love, far from it. Upon release, the club committee did not appreciate the album title 'The Queen Is Dead'. Like most conservative (with a small 'c') organizations, they found it discourteous and upsetting. The iconic photograph taken by Stephen Wright on the inner gatefold of the album features the band looking relaxed at the front door of an organisation built to defend King and Country. To the committee they would have seemed like barbarians at the (locked) gates. And Andy Rourke's smirk won't have helped their cause…

But this was Morrissey's Manchester; the Salford surroundings stored the sacred souls of his heroes. This was the reality in which his heroes were grounded. A turn of the century organisation built to improve the lot of the impoverished (and dangerous) working classes.

Over thirty years on and, thanks to that image, Salford Lads Club and The Smiths are forever linked. In truth

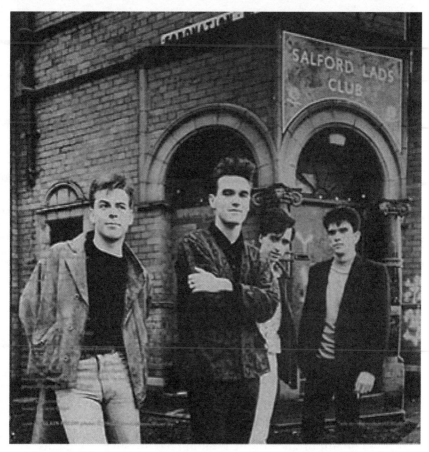

it probably began as a marriage of convenience. The club needed funds and, in the absence of new material, the fans needed a focal point; a place where their heroes stood and changed the world with a smirk.

The club slowly realised the possibilities as the fans kept coming. Initially shunned, they eventually opened their doors and accepted the pilgrims. Fans still flock to the club hoping that the sense of the soul of the Smiths remains. It's an essential stop on a tour of the city alongside the Holy Name Church and Cemetry (sic) Gates. As the sun and the clouds pass overhead, fans take turns and pass the camera "I'll be Morrissey, I'll be Johnny, I'll be Andy, I'll be Mike."

As Salford Lads Club project manager Leslie Holmes told

the BBC's Inside Out feature on the venue, "fans travel from Venezuela, Paraguay, Japan, Brazil, Chile, from all around the globe. The fans are very obsessive, they love Salford, the Smiths lyrics and the imagery, the music and appreciate everything about it". Eventually, the marriage provided an off-spring - a beautiful Smiths room within the club, covered in memorabilia, photographs and messages from fans.

This was a fantastic addition. The Smiths and their army of fans feel loved and welcomed. From a photo outside a building, to now, what feels like a welcoming hug as you walk through the door that leads to another place of pilgrimage and reflection. Inside the Salford Lads Club, you feel like a Salford lad, you feel like a Smith.

The fans now have a temple on the tracks, or a Vatican in the (V) alleyways. I feel this Edwardian fortress could sit well within Pere Lachaise cemetery – next to Wilde – celebrating life and what life leaves behind; it can recognise the end of the Smiths but more so it celebrates, so beautifully, the life of The Smiths. It seemed to be built for The Smiths.

The importance of the building has grown so much. In 2007, Morrissey donated money for repairs and Stephen Wright allowed one of his photographs from the infamous 1985 shoot to be reproduced onto a Lads Club T Shirt raising vital funds for the club. The money from the sales also enabled six young local people to travel to America as part of an exchange linked to the Salford Sioux Project

Leslie Holmes, told the *Manchester Evening News*, "I think fans will be delighted as we are by Morrissey's support. I imagine it is their dedication that made him aware of our cause and I hope his contribution will now alert others to it."

Leslie is the project manager at the heart of the Club

Okay, so Moz is here at 8pm…
I'll get here for 2pm the day before

A typical day (or two!) waiting for the gig

Some Moz rings

Tickets from around the globe, Boz plectrum and autographed box sets and, for some reason, a menu from the Grave Maurice

My Moz shirt and assorted memorabillia

Some memorabillia from my visit to Denmark.

Andrew Pares congratulates me on catchin Mozzer's shir

Jean-Paul's piece of Morrissey's orange shirt
and the keep sake he made with it

Delia's tickets and memorabillia

Paul's good luck note
for 'Leicester FC'

Patrick's postcard

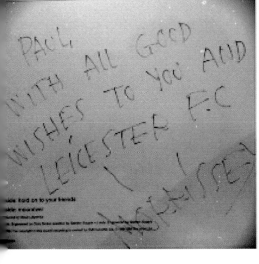

¡VIVA MORRISSEY! -Gustavo M.

Fender® MEDIUM 2011

Carol-Ann's hat as touched by the man himself

Adam and the guitar picks passed him by a security guard.

Arthur's waiting game pays off with a close-up!

Rocio gains an autograph but loses a friend.

*Aubrey's extensive
collection expands*

Jane reaches out…

Pete's piece of shirt

*Mick's autograph from
Boz and the band*

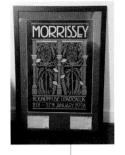

Kieran's prized possessions

Lorna suffers injury but creates a work of art.

Gary grabs a set list and a drumstick.

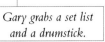

Gary's signed tambourine

Jurgen, lead singer of the best of The Smiths tribute acts

Josh on stage with Dallas based tribute band PANIC.

Harry Hill's signed fax from the man himself approving of his Stars In Their Eyes performance in 2004

Lisa's stage performances and lyrics have been inspired by a lifelong devotion to Morrissey and The Smiths

'Six nights at the same venue! Six nights of Moz in one straight hit! Six nights of him at his very best!' It's fair to say Jamie was thrilled with his 'Moz Season Ticket'

The welcoming arms of The Salford Lads Club has become a place of pilgrimage for Smiths devotees across the world. The club have responded by opening its doors and even devoting a room to memorabillia donated by visiting fans.

The MozBus tours came after author Phill Gatenby received repeated requests to show Smiths fans the sites he covered in his book 'Morrissey's Manchester'. Here fans visit Moz's family home in Stretford, the Iron Bridge and Strangeways as well as Salford Lads Club.

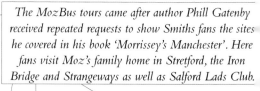

and is responsible for the gradual change in relationship between musical pilgrims and Salfordians. I asked him about the reaction of fans when they arrive there... "I see lots of people as they approach the building and it is brilliant to see the way they react. It's like people seeing the Taj Mahal or Times Square. It's something they have known all their lives but being there is both familiar and unique. I love it and when they realise they can come inside, it becomes even more special. We get lots of tears when people first go inside the Smiths room and that is even more special, it's why I have spent 14 years adding to it.

"I wanted the Smiths room to be a space inside the building for fans to leave a picture or a message. The intention is to show people that Salford Lads club is more than just a background to an album cover. I remember coming inside for the first time myself to do an arts project with local kids and I thought it was this most amazing place and it needed saving and the only way to do that is to get as many people as possible to visit and share this experience. It is one of the few surviving examples of a working class venue and remarkably it has kept every record, so for me it's of world heritage importance, otherwise we risk losing evidence of this kind of community."

So what impact have Smiths fans had on the club?

"The solidarity to keep the club open from an amazing group of volunteers, lads who came here aged 12, some of whom are now in their eighties. They have had a cast iron love and connection with the building, the club changed their lives and they want generation after generation to share those values. Stephen Wright and Morrissey wanting to take that picture in 1985 is another reason, it put the club on the map for a new audience, people who became fascinated by the place and wanted to share Morrissey's love of Shelagh Delaney, "A Taste of Honey" and how

Coronation Street emerged from her work. It has helped us raise a lot of money over the last 12 years to restore and improve the building, £1.5 million at the last count."

Leslie adds that The Smiths are not the only Manchester band with a connection to the club, "Well, when Rough Trade rang the club to ask permission to take the photo in 1985, the volunteer who answered the phone asked if it was the Hollies who wanted their picture taking! We get fans of a certain generation calling in and they like the idea that Graham Nash and Alan Clarke came up from the ranks here, learning to play banjos and harmonicas, so it has an audience and it's part of the history here, but unfortunately there was no Stephen Wright around at the time and we have no pictures of them here as The Hollies, or the Guy Tones as they were first known. Their image was not centred around Salford, a few song titles, but I don't know of any local images of them which is a pity.

"Over the years local people accept the occasional invasion of Smiths fans as part of daily life, I've seen lots of local people helping out taking photos of fans so I think it's a great relationship. It also means people don't overreact to famous musicians or celebrities, they just take it for granted. The publicity that we get is a lifeline for the club, because it brings so many different audiences here and everybody loves it, I think we look at lots of ideas of events that people want to put on here, and we are careful about what we do, it has to be something that is sympathetic to the building or is something different or unusual, it's brilliant and long may it continue."

In many ways The Salford Lads Club stands for so much more than other iconic images such as Abbey Road. The photograph represents Morrissey's inspirations; his poetry, the North, and a local community filled with characters good, bad or indifferent. His inspirations.

THE MOZBUS

See Plate 8

Such is the association of fans with the various sites mentioned in Morrissey's lyrics that taking people around Manchester and London to view the places namechecked in his songs spawned a cottage industry. Avid fan and author Phill Gatenby explains....

The MozBus made its debut in time for the Morrissey 'comeback' gig at the MEN Arena in May 2004. It wasn't an original idea – in the late 80's and early 90's there had been a couple of Smiths conventions at the students union at Manchester University that had included a tour on a bus.

My tour guide, 'Morrissey's Manchester', had been published by Empire Publications in 2002 and up until the gig I had not done any private tours for fans – to be honest, I don't think I was asked to do any, the whole point of the book was for people to undertake it themselves. However, when the gig was announced, requests came in for me to put something on. Originally I planned for the Saturday afternoon and paid a deposit on a coach (that had to have a microphone so I could talk) and a CD player!

I took payment via cheques on a first come, first served basis. A few overseas fans struggled to pay and promised to turn up on the day but having paid out on the deposit, I needed to know I had covered my costs before taking the chance on someone hopefully turning up.

It soon became clear that a second tour would be required as numbers exceeded fifty very quickly, so I booked another trip on the night before the gig and gave fans who had already booked the choice of which trip they wanted – the Friday night or the Saturday afternoon.

A bit of planning had to go into the tour – liaising with Salford Lads Club around timing of arrivals and writing to the Governor of HMP Strangeways, asking for approval of turning up with fifty fans and standing outside the old gates! The Governor replied positively, stating that he would place the book I sent him in the prison library for the 'residents' to enjoy! I was informed that the prison was a high security unit and no one was to take pictures of the outside walls, of cameras situated on the walls or of people coming and going from the reception – just keep focused on the old gates and there would not be a problem! The letter from the Governor came in handy several times over the following years when doing private tours as the security van would quickly come around to see who was hanging around the old gates! For every MozBus after this one, I always sent a courtesy letter out, giving the date and time the bus would arrive and there was never a problem.

I was also contacted by the *NME*, who had found out about the trip and wanted to send a reporter and photographer on the Saturday trip. Permission granted. It was amazing, that as an avid reader of the *NME* since the age of 15, that there I was... given a whole page at the age of 41!

So the day of the tours arrived. The vast majority of the Friday night trip were European and Saturday afternoon they were American. So the beer I was selling on the bus ran out by the time we'd got to Southern Cemtery on the Friday night – yet I only sold half of the beer on the Saturday lunchtime, getting strange looks from American fans as if to say "It's 1pm.... why would we want a beer?"

The Friday trip was great; there was a fantastic atmosphere on board and everyone was dropped off at the Star & Garter, who were hosting the Smiths disco. However, the Saturday trip turned out to be rather special.

The Lads Club had tipped me off that Andy Rourke and Vinny Peculiar would play a special acoustic set and I kept this to myself, saying there would be a special treat in store at some point today! Upon arrival at the Lads Club, Linder Sterling was there filming and taking pictures of fans – that appeared on the 'extras' on the ''Who Put The M In Manchester'' DVD of the gig that she herself produced. I noticed her straight away, gave a little knowing nod and carried on as everyone else walked past her, oblivious as to who she was. Within time her cover was blown and everyone was keen to speak with her and thanking me for arranging this special treat that I had mentioned! I had to own up that this was not the treat I was referring to and I had no idea she was turning up.

Once inside the club I was asked to introduce the special guests which was a privilege. The pair performed five songs, three of which were Smiths covers, including ''Bigmouth'', where Vinny updated and changed the lyric to "and her Ipod started to melt" (something Morrissey himself sang a few years later!). Our time in the Lads Club was supposed to be around forty minutes but had become an hour and a half so off we ventured to the rest of the tour with the NME on board, stalking our every move. The tour, in order of visit, stopped at Parkers Hotel (back cover of Strangeways album), HMP Strangeways, Salford Lads Club, 384 Kings Road, The Iron Bridge, Southern Cemetery, The Holy Name Church and ended where it all began – The Ritz.

The tours had taken their toll on me.... Friday evening's tour followed by the Star & Garter (getting home at 3am full of alcohol) and up at 10am for the next tour (and not eating much throughout the day) had me feeling that I would be too shattered to be at the gig itself and I had pushed myself too far with two tours. The tours are mentally exhausting

rather than physically exhausting... making sure everyone is on board and not left at the cemetery (like four fans were on the Saturday!) dealing with the coach driver, who is stating if another stone is thrown at the coach (outside the Lads Club) from a local kid then he is leaving! Then there was the one fan who found a pigeon injured outside the Lads Club and asked if I had the number for the RSPCA (I kid you not...) I have the driver threatening to leave and a fan wanting to save a pigeon whilst also looking out for forty nine other fans too ...The pigeon saver somehow got the number from inside the Lads Club and when no one answered, asked me if we could divert to take the pigeon to the RSPCA.... I didn't know who I wanted to strangle more.... the pigeon or the fan... needless to say we went on our way eventually with a relieved driver and a pigeon free bus.

Of course, when the bus did arrive at Salford Lads Club, there would always be many, many other fans there too, who had made their own way there independently – some of whom would try and catch a free ride on the onward journey. That is why I produced lanyard tickets – no lanyard, no ride! On the bus itself, I have fifty punters that want to chat with me, which is great, you try and share yourself around them all but know that some dominant characters will get more than their fair share of my time than others – you want each fan to have the same experience but know that cannot happen with fifty people and three and a half hours to do it all – and that is a little disappointing. After the Saturday tour had finished, I went home and from 4pm to 6.30pm, I slept. Woke up and got a bus into town and felt refreshed – once the gig started, the adrenalin was more than enough to keep my legs holding up the rest of my body!

I ran two more MozBus tours – a few months later

before The Move Festival at Lancashire County Cricket ground (altering the route to end up at the venue) and before Morrissey's 50th birthday in 2009 when I hired Sankey Soap's Disco Bus - a double decker bus with a few seats downstairs so punters can dance on the dance floor on their way back home at 3am! Holding seventy passengers, I managed to squeeze (literally) ninety on it - with the driver given a generous 'bonus' at the end!

A few weeks after the 2004 gig, I received the odd email asking if I would undertake a personal tour as they were visiting Manchester and wanted to see the sites. I don't know why but I somehow felt obliged and I charged a tenner (same price if there was one fan or four), which really just covered petrol and a pint afterwards. I never saw it as a money making thing, just something I enjoyed doing. It was always the American visitors who told me I was undercharging! As much as the bus tours were fun, I much preferred the personal tours as there was less rushing around, less stress and I had a lot more time to chat with the punters. Interestingly, I would say most of the trips were with females or couples where the female was the fan and the partner was being dragged around these unlikely tourist destinations.

One of the most memorable trips was with Diane from Brooklyn (who remains a good friend to this day and we have met up at many gigs since, both in the UK and the USA) who came over with her husband. My car had broken down but I offered to do the tour via public transport! We got the bus from the city centre to the Holy Name Church, then another one onto Southern Cemetery and then a third bus alighting at the beginning of Kings Road in Stretford. This was a Sunday and the bus here was once every hour and we had just missed it.... so on we walked to the Iron Bridge, then 384 Kings Road and then onto Salford Lads Club on foot (via lunch in a pub next to Manchester United's ground – much to my annoyance!) We then began walking to Strangeways from the Lads Club and half way there a friend of mine driving by spotted us, turned round, picked us up and dropped us at the prison gates!

After numerous requests to do a London version of Morrissey's Manchester (turned down because I didn't know all of the places and assumed / hoped someone from London would do it) I finally relented and spent time researching places and then making three trips totalling eight days where I walked all points of the compass of the capital in order to produce "Panic On The Streets" which came out in 2007. When Morrissey announced six concerts over a seven night period at The Roundhouse in Camden (January 2008), the chance to do a tour of London sites was mentioned and The MozTube was born, taking place on the Thursday – the one day when there was not a gig scheduled.

Purchasing an all day pass, seventeen of us started off from Euston Station and headed for the Grave Maurice pub in Whitechapel, the leaning post at Tench Street/ Reardon Street in Wapping and the close by Turks Head pub. Then there was Sloane Square, the 'Suedehead' house, Geales Fish Restaurant in Notting Hill, Piccadilly Circus and The Rock Garden venue – home of The Smiths first London gig (and now an Apple Store!) We even walked from the tube station to Vallance Street – where the Kray twins grew up in Bethnall Green – only to find the street sign where Morrissey once posed under had gone. It was there when I did the book, honest!

It was a long day but really enjoyable – we even lost a couple at one very busy station where the doors closed before they could get on.... they caught up with us some forty minutes later but a budding romance developed between them (did they miss that train on purpose?) and last I heard they were engaged!

So I had undertaken the tours on a coach, car and using public transport above and underground. But the best tour of them all was on a bicycle. In 2007, it was reported (with no sense of irony lost) that Salford Lads Club had been the victim of thieves stealing lead from the roof. A suggestion was made for fans to raise money and as a result "Bigmouth Bikes Again" was born. The aim was to cycle the sixteen miles from the Lads Club to 384 Kings Road, the Iron Bridge, Southern Cemetery, The Holy Name Church, Strangeways (letter to the Governor sent!) and back to the Lads Club. A total of just over seventy riders took part from all over the country and two from the USA. Setting off on a glorious late October Sunday morning, with local MP Hazel Blears and papier mache star Frank Sidebottom cutting the ribbon and sending us off on our way, we returned to be entertained by tribute band The Smyths – giving their time for free, having played a gig in Birkenhead the night before. There was a wonderful atmosphere throughout the day which was covered by the local BBC and Granada News teams The BBC had said they would follow the entire tour for a report for the following days' edition providing Granada were nowhere in sight! So as fellow organiser Ruth was being interviewed by the Beeb at the front of the building, I was cheekily holding court with Granada at the back of the building. The BBC kept to their word and were waiting at each site and produced a very good account of the day over a four minute feature.

The trips for many, especially overseas fans, where a once in a lifetime trip or the end of searching for the Holy Grail. So many excited faces and fulfilled dreams made the trips very enjoyable – sometimes they got a little emotional....There was one women, Canadian I think, and she warned me when we met that things might get a little tearful. The visit to Parkers Hotel and HMP Strangeways offered no clues as to what would follow. Upon arriving at the Lads Club I was informed that "I just need a little time to myself" and I left her in the car at the side of the building and went inside to meet up with Leslie Holmes.

Ten minutes later I went back to the car and she was just getting out of it, bracing herself for that moment when she walked around to the front and caught sight of the iconic sign above the door. She managed to hold it together long enough for me to take the picture. That was nothing though to the tears shed upon reaching 384 Kings Road... she had planned a trip for over fifteen years and was simply overwhelmed by finally achieving her dream to visit all the sights. When Manchester City won the FA Cup in 2011, I cried tears of joy and emotion as Carlos Tevez hoisted the trophy high – and it made me recall the Canadian fan and her reaction on her dream coming true after fifteen years. My wait had been thirty-five years!

One of my favourite jokes to play on the MozBus, was when approaching the Lads Club. To be able to park outside the front of the club, you had to drive past it on Regent Road for about a quarter of a Mike and then enter the estate via a side street and follow it around to the club. Just before we would pass the club, I would grab the microphone and say "If everyone looks to the left at the end of this row of houses, you will see Salford Lads Club". The gap opened up and upon site of the club, everyone would give a cheer or an "ahhh" and then I would add "OK, that was the Lads Club, next stop is Kings Road" and sit back down to half laughter and half gasps of disbelief!

By now I had become a victim of my own success. The more personal tours I did, the more word spread and more bookings took place. The tours had outgrown me. I was working Monday to Friday and also had my daughters at weekends, plus watching Manchester City every other weekend August to May. It was at this point that the Inspiral Carpets drummer, Craig Gill, got in touch, indicating that he wanted to start up a business running music tours beyond The Smiths & Morrissey – featuring Joy Division/ New Order/Factory Records and the Stone Roses, Oasis, punk and much more. Craig wanted to take what I was doing as a 'thing on the side' to another level.

Craig succeeded – but that, is another story...

THE CHURCH OF MOZ?

PIECES OF MORRISSEY

Since I began this project, several aspects have stood out; the language that fans have used in discussing all aspects of their memorabilia. The location of where the items are displayed. And the emotional or financial value of the memorabilia to the fan.

This led me to investigate studies or reports in behaviours in fandom and obsession. Although the reports and studies are not directly aimed at me – they concern my behaviour among the realms of 'fandom' and 'obsession'. It's difficult studying your own behaviour and whether people think it's natural, normal or kind, however, the more I read from the fans the more I thought, is it really so strange?

Language

For me the comforting and almost celebratory words "I have Morrissey's shirt" has entered into regular conversation. In discussion with fans of music, or anyone in general really, I usually discuss my adulation for Morrissey and I usually finalise the sentence with "I have Morrissey's shirt, it's my prized possession" or, "it means the world to me".

For years, I've spent time telling people, whether they are interested or not (and they are usually not) that I am proud to be a Morrissey fan and now it seems I have a bolt on. I have to inform them I have his shirt - a Piece of Morrissey. I've mentioned this so often, that there has almost been a change in my identity as I've overheard people saying, "that's Matty, Matt or Matthew – he has Morrissey's shirt" my surname has disappeared, is it time to change the name on my passport?

My shirt and my pieces of Morrissey are of huge value.

While I have the records and other memorabilllia, the shirt was, for many years, unattainable. I could never buy the shirt of Morrissey. No one has ever sold such an item in a shop. Probe records or HMV didn't branch out that far. And, if they did, I don't think I would have bought one. I wanted the experience of Morrissey wearing it then launching it into the crowd – to me. It has a personal touch, the story of how it was obtained is a personal experience recalling the feeling, excitement and frenzy of the moment.

Some artists that appear on Twitter or Facebook regularly give away items. But, I think, although good for the fan, this reduces the exclusivity or importance of the memorabilia, but for them it works – it's not for everyone. What I have is a perfect history and perfect memorabilia. I was at the gig, I was there, enjoying the gig and I was lucky to go home with a piece of Morrissey.

This project has confirmed to me not only the strength, pull and adulation of Morrissey but also the desire to have a piece of Him. When I closely review the language used by fans in discussing their memorabilia, it is very interesting to see how fans describe memorabilia, what it means to them or how they managed to retrieve the item.

Feedback from fans and tales indicate personalities change when the chance of jumping on stage for a Mozhug, or a chance to go home with a piece of memorabilia or an autograph is in sight. I sensed there was no backing down – nothing was too dangerous; just a hearty, passionate, warrioresque, grit and determination from MozArmy footsoldiers to obtain their piece of the man. In conversation, or via email, fans used language such as: "I was determined, it had to be mine, it was mine", "it was a matter of life or death, I couldn't let go of it", "Morrissey threw it to me, I know he did".

Others have openly admitted, "I'm usually timid, but

on this occasion, I wasn't going to be pushed or stopped by anyone, a handshake from Morrissey was my aim. I felt I could live my life after this handshake, so no man or woman would have stopped me". Then there are the battles with stage security, "The security guard may have been six foot seven, each way, but look I'm feisty, just not very often in the real world, but this was the moment to be feisty – I gently persuaded the guy to move out the way".

Someone else admitted, "The frenzy for the piece of the shirt is such a frenzy because it's Morrissey, no other artist would have this impact, I can't see people scrambling over Bono's, or Chris Martin's shirt, I had to take it home, he makes me who I am , he completes me. I don't conform to anything because of Morrissey". Another regular refrain is "I'll never sell it, never ever ever" and "It changed my life – this is a religion, so maybe I wanted my religious relic".

Of course, lives change for many reasons; from changing schools, jobs, marriage, divorce, children, death, law, and events out of our control such as political upheavals or natural disasters. But clearly this personal statement from honest and open fans indicates the object of, or from, Morrissey could be just as important as all of the above. It's certain that their life was enhanced because of it. Lives have changed, no one has minded and everyone was appreciative. I know I am certainly grateful.

But Morrissey and 'religion' is another avenue to explore, or at least dip into with a cautious toe. A high percentage of fans used, or suggested, a connotation or a religious connection using language like worship, belief, faith and sacred with their devotions to the Church of Moz.

"I Have Forgiven Religion"

Religion is generally defined as 'a cultural system of behaviours and practices, world views, ethics, and social organisation that relate humanity to an order of existence' – or so I'm told. And before you write to Points of View to point your view, I'm aware there are numerous definitions of religions. Defining the word "Religion" is fraught in itself. Many attempts have been made people focus on a very narrow definition that matches the individual's own religion.

To me, 'religion' is a word that has many meanings, many connotations and many areas of concern. I am not clever enough, smart enough, brave enough, or clued up enough to discuss in depth, the realms and boundaries of religion without treading on delicate toes – it wouldn't be deliberately offensive of me, it'd just be naïve, so I won't dip in to it too much. But we all have beliefs of one sort or another and with everything, we also have concerns. It seems there are more religions than people in the world. I truly hope that "Love, Peace and Harmony should be the common goal" but I don't think it is.

This word 'religion' appeared many times in fans feedback and in discussion over Morrissey. It also had an extra friend as the word 'relic' often joined the debate as fans compared memorabilia to religious relics. I recognise what fans are indicating. I too feel the fandom is something above the norm. It is Morrissey after all, it's bound to be above the norm.

But is 'Religion' an apt expression of the level of commitment? Are we right to use it? Wrong to use it? And does it really matter? I'm not going to answer yes or no. I'll let you do that. I'll just throw a few things light heartedly from the tree and see how they land in your garden, would you Adam and Eve I'd do that ?

For me, it does seem something very strong and maybe running parallel to the fandom and obsession. There is a huge amount of worship to the mythological archetype located on the peak of Mount Morrissey. Lyrical couplets are beautifully scripted and pronounced to the adoring army below. Morrissey interprets and articulates life so accurately to his eager and dedicated disciples that they have an emotional impact, making sense of their world, their reality. They are open and honest scriptures, not about the meek inheriting the earth but about the earth being the loneliest planet of all. Suddenly life makes sense to the believer, Moz has explained a condition of modern life and love as if to say, 'you are not alone'.

Non-Morrissey fans can, and usually do, let me know in no certain terms that I'm talking crap; it's not a religion, it's a cult with his fans following their leader too far up his bleep bleep bleep. Yet, Moz fans use the term religion freely. After all Morrissey fandom has a system of behaviours, views, ethics and there are levels of commitment, love and dedication. Fans described their dedicated holidays to visit the Salford Lads Club, or Morrissey's old home as a "pilgrimage" - a word typically used for a journey to a shrine, or area or location of importance. But, to Morrissey fans, these locations are important as they hold moral or spiritual significance. You must please remember - Morrissey has been there. Not only that but he has referred to these places in his lyrics, he has been there and been inspired! Want to visit the Cemetry Gates (sic) – no problem, here's a map and a guide book. However, to compare it with a religious site in Jerusalem might seem ridiculous, but is it? Perhaps the MozArmy is smaller in number and membership is not passed down from father to son but some might seem just as fanatical...

Of course, it is not just Morrissey fans that use the term religion. BBCTV's 'Inside Out' produced a wonderful, sensitive and respectful film on Morrissey and the MozArmy. In the introduction the presenter says, "Fans flock to see the place that inspired the songs of influential 80s band, The Smiths. Their lead singer Morrissey, once a shy young man writing lyrics in his bedroom, has now achieved iconic status. He's fêted around the globe with the kind of passion usually reserved for boy bands. The kind of fervour displayed at Morrissey gigs is approaching religious proportions"

The BBC say "it's approaching," some fans say it has made it, but either way, religion is quoted and used by those fans or the media. Whether it's right or wrong is open to interpretation.

Memorabilia, artefact or religious relic?

Fans have used the word 'relic' to describe their pieces of Morrissey. To highlight their devotion, commitment and dedication. Yet is that going too far? Would 'artefact' suffice? Should we drop the religious aspect and just have relic? Is 'cultural relic' apt?

A relic is also the term for something that has survived the passage of time, especially an object or custom whose original culture has disappeared, but also an object cherished for historical or memorial value; keepsakes or heirlooms. Add this explanation to my tiny piece of shirt from my first gig in 1990 and my full shirt from 2009 and hey Presto, it's a cultural relic!

If fans class items as religious relics, would it cause outrage? I hope not. Language is here for a reason and like anyone else, fans have a right to express how they feel about Morrissey and his memorabilia. And if Morrissey is a religion to some then the memorabilia is a relic of this religion.

But again, I'm not saying what is right or wrong or what we should or shouldn't do. I'll leave that to you.

Are relics really so strange?

If fans class their obsession as a religion and their memorabilia as religious relics or artifacts, (oh hang on, before we do – do we need a stamp of authority and approval?) should it be disregarded by others? Or is it right that it is seen as an odd obsession, like trainspotting or morris dancing. You know, silly Morrissey fans being silly about silly ideas, in their silly bedrooms, being all silly about so called silly relics.

I am not talking about former possessions like my old television from 1987; which is located in the garage. A garage I haven't been in since 1987; a TV with buttons as big as the garage door that could break a finger when pressed. It was once a prized possession, presumably in the weeks following its purchase some time in the 70s. Then it became a part of the family, the events witnessed through it are memorable to me at any rate. There's nothing religious about it obviously but I used to watch it until the dot disappeared for good. I miss that dot. I used to enjoy watching it. Would I react to it differently if it had been Morrissey's telly?

Artefacts have made the world spin around for years. Silly relics celebrated around our globe – there are museums dedicated to the "odd as a box of frogs" artefact. And after witnessing these items I'm starting to believe we certainly have a case to define and celebrate memorabilia however we wish; relic, artefact or religious relic.

The days of old paintings and historic artefacts are gone, so much so that Time Magazine ran a spread with alluring headlines

"Check out six of the weirdest artefacts found in New York museum collections, including one of Anthony Weiner's sexting transcripts at the Museum of Sex. You'll never look at the mayoral hopeful the same way again."

Which is a good job I don't look at him at all – ever. Furthermore, there are Museums dedicated around the world to:

Icelandic Phallological Museum
Reykjavik, Iceland

If the name didn't tip you off, this museum is dedicated to all things penile. According to its website, it houses more than 215 penises and penile parts belonging to almost all the land and sea mammals found in Iceland. Be sure not to miss the special section dedicated to whale penises.

Be sure to miss it… .that's my Tripadvisor tip.

The Museum of Bad Art
Brookline and Somerville, Massachusetts, USA

Known as MOBA for short, this museum touts itself as "the world's only museum dedicated to the collection, preservation, exhibition and celebration of bad art in all its forms." Why waste your time at art museums showcasing quality art, that will only makes you feel untalented? As you stroll through MOBA, you'll grow more and more confident about your own artistic abilities. All the pieces "range from the work of talented artists that have gone awry to works of exuberant, although crude, execution by artists barely in control of the brush."

I'm on my way with my matchstick Matt and Moz drawings

Sulabh International Museum of Toilets
New Delhi, India

Ever wanted to learn about the evolution of toilets throughout human history? Then get yourself to India to visit this museum, which traces the history of the toilet for the past 4,500 years. From simple chamber pots to elaborate decorated Victorian toilet seats, you'll see it all. There's even a toilet disguised as a bookcase.

And a Toilet disguised as a Museum.

Avanos Hair Museum
Avanos, Turkey

Want a creepier option than toilets, penises and bad art? Look no further than this hair museum created by potter Chez Galip, in the rural Turkish town of Avanos. It features a huge collection of hair gathered from more than 16,000 women, and if that doesn't sound creepy enough for you: it's situated in a small, dark cave.

I do hope the 16000 women were asked to donate this and it wasn't a drive by chopping.

The Museum of Broken Relationships.
~~(It's in my flat!)~~ Zagreb, Croatia

This museum evolved "from a travelling exhibition revolving around the concept of failed relationships and their ruins," their website explains. Visitors are encouraged to donate artefacts from their own broken relationships as "a chance to overcome an emotional collapse." You'll see obvious artefacts; rings, clothing, Valentine's Day gifts — but you'll also spot some stranger remnants like fuzzy pink handcuffs or a wooden watermelon.

I'll be sending over the "Matt you are dumped cards" from 1985, '87 , '90 & '93, '94, '96, '97…

After reading the above; I don't think it should be too much of a problem to class our memorabilia the way we wish. We have our treasure – and thankfully ours is here to stay, but.....

Everything's Lost

Let's celebrate the fact we still have these Moz items! Let's not just display them, let's tell people we have them. Shout loud and proud what they mean to you, to us. Throw down the codes and rules for the day and hop, skip and jump down the road to buy some Moz bunting and celebrate with a great big slice of whoop de whoop Moz cake at the fact you still have them in your possession. Because things can get a little bit lost... forever.

Despite a collector's world and a world of impulse buying, we've still managed to lose some pretty big things in time – not me and you by the way; we lose keys, mobile phones, cash cards, train tickets, even our marbles and the ever so important remote control, every other day. But, things have been so culturally important the tag "priceless" is almost an undervaluation. The following items have been lost. Basically, it's a list of the lost and never ever to be found.

The year, 1856, 29 May, Bloomington, Illinois. Abraham Lincoln took to the stage and delivered a 90-minute firebrand address. This speech established the Illinois Republican Party. It pushed Lincoln into the limelight and set the course for Civil War, Reconstruction, and the creation of modern America. And no copy of it is known to exist – so please check the back of your couch.

We roughly know what the speech was about as someone at the meeting listened and they also wrote it down on a scrap of paper. But they didn't write down a full account of it. Or a full accurate copy of what was really said that night does not exist. By all accounts, it's alleged, Lincoln simply spoke a collection of heartfelt words that then vanished into the atmosphere.

The speech, which contained some pretty hardnosed, brutal views on slavery, may have been deliberately censored by Lincoln to ward off accusations of extremism. Whatever the reason, it remains possibly Lincoln's greatest speech and the only one you'll never have the chance to study – but it gets a mention here at least. Missing account, missing memorabilia and by all account - missing memories.

In 1942, director Orson Welles was just slowly arriving back on earth from the high rise Citizen Kane and commenced on a new project. Orson turned his attention to a prize-winning, but nearly forgotten novel called The Magnificent Ambersons. He promptly produced a masterpiece that modern critics have labelled 'stronger and better than Kane'. And these critics say this without even seeing the full film—the studio destroyed nearly a third of it – the end of it. Welles was called away on war work to South America and while he was away studio bosses butchered his epc and changed the ending; his moving, 132-minute elegy to the America of his youth was shredded and the missing bits dumped at sea. Polluting the seabed but, giving those little fishies and dolphins some classic memorabilia.

And no doubt, the Hollywood wayward way will transpire to the world and the Orcas will be recreating Orson at the next Seasick world show. Seasick world often tell us Orcas are happy to dance every hour to 'Walking on Sunshine' or Michael Jackson's 'Thriller' – but, it's a sad sad world and full of lies. I've seen it, I cried. I protested. I was told 'if you don't like it Sir you can go, you can leave the park.' So I did.

For Welles, the entire first half and a new ending still exist, the picture that could have been the greatest movie ever made has gone to sleep on the seabed. Memorabilia in watered down pieces.

In 1888, the 'From Hell' letter, a note purporting to be from Jack the Ripper to London police. It arrived in a box that also contained half a human kidney, and it was considered to possibly be the only authentic communication from history's most notorious serial killer. And as ever, at some point, the police managed to lose both it and the kidney it came with. The implications were huge, no doubt the police didn't blame themselves. Don't ever blame them – just get yourself back to the ghetto. Of course, modern techniques would have allowed us to confirm whether the kidney came from one of Jack's victims. If it had, we could validate the letter itself. Secondly, it's always possible some trace may have been left on the paper, potentially allowing us to finally solve the Whitechapel murders. Instead, this vital element was either stolen or thrown away, leaving us as stumped as the Victorians were. If it hasn't been stolen, this artefact may still exist.

Finally if you're going to lose something, you might as well lose something big. That's the logic our species has seemingly applied to the Margites, an ancient epic written by Greek poet Homer. According to several ancient sources, Homer wrote the Margites before the more famous and surviving Iliad and Odyssey. It was apparently very good, with Aristotle claiming that it basically invented Greek comedy. And since the Iliad is now routinely called the "first great book" and the first work of Western literature; that means, the honour should instead have gone to the missing and no doubt tearful Margites. No doubt it has a speech prepared just in case the awards come calling. In other words, finding this lost comedy wouldn't just give us a new book by one of history's greatest authors. It would involve resetting the entire Western canon to start with it.

In their rundown of missing books, the Smithsonian called it the greatest work "you'll never have a chance to read," a fitting epitaph for Western literature's very first item but I could say something similar about a book I once wrote and lost – no, not this one.

These items of course are seen as priceless, it's fascinating to see how the human race can let us down. The human race is pretty good at it too. But, during my project what didn't let me down was the MozArmy and their tales. MozArmy treasured items are here to stay. If a fan managed to lose their prized possession, I wouldn't like to be in the same room as the fan, there would be bloodshed on the streets as reports of the missing items are fed to newsreels around this globe. Morrissey fans are passionate and aware of what they have and what it means. We will always try to keep the items safe under lock and key.

For Morrissey fans, the event doesn't have to happen for it to be celebrated! As fans even celebrate concerts that were cancelled. Feedback sent to me show that fans have tickets in frames from concerts that never happened! Some kept hold of the ticket that was never ripped on entry, or its bar code scanned. Fans retained the full ticket. I was intrigued by this as I have one or two full tickets myself – from Camden Roundhouse. I don't display them, but I think I might now.

It even triggered off a question or two to the fans and I asked if they felt the ticket is celebrating a show that may have been the finest of them all? Most agreed, confirming that quite often the expectation can outshine the actual event. There seemed to be no room for debate. Fans felt it was a quirky, unique item. And some felt Morrissey was due to play there so that was enough. I know, I understand, I once said "I'd pay £50 to be in the same city as Morrissey". I just don't know the city he is in. But my £50 is ready.

To the devoted, Morrissey religiously fights for human/animal rights and social justice. And the fans will religiously be there with him fighting for human / animal rights and social justice. Morrissey's songs, voice and lyrics have altered the path of existence for myself and millions of others across the globe. But, for many, the retrieval of memorabilia shifted the path again. As, the memorabilia changed their lives and their homes.

Location Location Location – Who cares?

The location of the memorabilia, or where it's stored or displayed, is another interesting point to discuss. The location really triggered off a reaction from non-fans and fans regarding the whereabouts of items on display in homes across the globe.

Ideas of the home are historically shaped, culturally informed and open to debate. Historically, the home was seen as a paradox of imaginative retreat from the world and as a place that signified personal identity. The home has also been seen as a changing dynamic as the use of the home changed in time as technology, originally used in the outside world, crept into the home.

There is evidence that individual / families across society bought the knick-knacks; vases, pictures or ornaments to express their identity, lifestyle, wealth, culture, and pride in their home. It also enhanced their experience or retreat from the workplace. Historically, most homes have bought into the trend of buying the ornaments, or the glass cabinet, the decanters, the crystal glasses that lurks just behind the sparkling glass cabinets which sits just to the left of the gleaming gold objet d'art. I've seen it, I've lived in it – I've been swamped in it.

Decorating the home defines a personality, a culture and a person. It still continues, these days it often becomes an obsession with owning the latest technology; the new, upgraded, top of the range, plasma television of all sizes and expense. The size range can go from televisions the size of a 'television', to televisions the size of Coventry. Plasma HD Ace/Fab/Top banana-blah de blah blurb televisions hang with pride as the family sit 4 miles away to focus in on another gloomy episode of EastEnders. It may display wealth, it may display consumer activity in extravagance but Morrissey has also put a block to this.

What is fascinating is consumer activity in technology, knick-knacks, ornaments and Morrissey. From all the brands around the world, small brands to leading brands, fans have expressed their individual decor choice at home – is Morrissey. Fans' décor is a memory of him and his memorabilia.

MY ROOM WITH A VIEW...
OF MORRISSEY

To others, the location of my items increased my level of adulation, fandom and obsession for Morrissey. As mentioned, I have my very own MozzerLiver Birds in my bedroom. I thought it was natural place to display them, but the reaction of non-Morrissey fans was different. People thought there was something wrong with this – but why? It's my room. And the shirts don't keep me awake snoring? Or sleepwalking. I have my desk, my music and my Morrissey collection in my room – so why shouldn't it be there? I didn't question what they kept in their bedrooms, I don't really want to know. And I'm too scared to ask. But, a bedroom is a room with a bed and now it includes a shirt that belonged to Morrissey.

Over the years, people asked where I store, or how I display the shirt. Simply, I bought two tailor's dummies; one for the shirt and one for the T shirt from the 'Everyday is Like Sunday' video. They usually enquire – for how much? I answer £140 to proudly display my two items, but the shirt from the gig is my ultimate treasured item. "You must be mad!" Is the usual reply. "I'm not – it's Morrissey and when I look at the shirt, I still see Morrissey in it, I still hear the voice, the songs, the band, the crowd, the applause and the doors swinging as I ran out of the theatre with Morrissey's shirt down my trousers – it's my piece of Morrissey".

"Not must be, you are mad!" they confirm with minimal analysis. They are not being rude or nasty, they just do not comprehend the adulation. They all have interests, whether it be music or sport, but maybe they are yet to understand what we as Morrissey fans cherish and adore, but they will. One day – one day.

I'm still unsure if they were concerned for the financial aspect. But, I shop Moz, therefore I am. I still paid my mortgage, I still travel to work, I still eat (granted wine and biscuits – but that's my staple diet). It seems fandom could be understood, but the issue of displaying items in the home took their confusion to a different level. However, my items will remain where they are; standing tall, powerful and poignant.

Narratives and stories received from fans also indicate they store their memorabilia in a wide range of locations around the house or on themselves. As pieces of Morrissey's shirt have been sown into clothes, scarves, jackets and jumpers. Or pieces of shirts attached to musical instruments or even bedposts or lamps. Or, they are now attached to a ticket stub in a frame.

Photographs and autographs are stored in wallets or carefully placed in frames and situated all around living rooms, kitchens and bedrooms or the work place, and even sent across to families and friends across the world. Tambourines go on display alongside family items and heirlooms. Or alongside family photos and cherished mementos they have framed their picture of Morrissey; their favourite album, poster or magazine cutting. Other fans who have managed to retrieve drumsticks display these in expensive frames and locate them strategically above the fireplace with a note to indicate the time the place they managed to retrieve their memorabilia.

Feedback has suggested that fan memorabilia is as important as the furniture the family sit on, or the family cooking essentials, or even family mementos. There is a place for everything and for many, Morrissey sits in that place, there Morrissey sits at home with fans at breakfast, dinner, birthdays and Xmas – now there is a thought.

There is another aspect of memorabilia that is deep rooted into personalities and personal appearance. It lodges deep into the skin. Attached to a limb, it can travel from room to room in minutes, from city to city in hours, or from supermarket to supermarket pushing a trolley and go from A to B on a train - after moments of pain. It is the Moz tattoo.

I am yet to get a Morrissey tattoo but I have friends who have suffered the pain. I'm suitably impressed they have chosen to place Morrissey's signature, lyric, portrait or Morrissey inspired design, not on a piece of paper, but on a part of the body. A part they and their loved ones will look at every day of their lives. It's a remarkable gesture. I've never been fortunate enough to meet Morrissey for the autograph. One day, I may ask for the pen to meet the skin. I may ask for a signature on the arm or the letter 'M' on the wrist, but I know my luck too well, I fear my luck will be issued with a P45 and become redundant as I nervously lose my marbles (again) and ask something ridiculous "erm erm erm you ever reclaimed PPI Moz?" and I'll forget to ask for the autograph. But Stetsons off to those who have met Morrissey and have his name scratched on your arm with a tattoo pen. Devotion is your middle name.

My home, and the homes of the MozArmy have been invaded – by Morrissey, well not so much invaded – we opened the door and invited him in. It is Morrissey, his memorabilia and memories. And that's all that matters, it means the world to fans, the value is emotional and that cannot be valued.

"SELL, SELL, SELL"

The language used by fans confirms the financial meaning of memorabilia. I have encountered on numerous occasions, the assured financial statement.

"I will not sell – for any price".

"I'd miss the item."

"I'd gain nothing by selling."

"I could do with extra money but I'd lose something bigger, I'd lose part of me"

"Morrissey signed it for me – not for me to sell it"

I understand, I wouldn't sell my shirt, in fact it's coming with when I go wherever I go. It's not just a shirt, it's not just the concert at the Empire, it's 27 years of adulation, emotions, soul, understanding - a connection, love and it's part of me. It holds an aura – it displays a soul. I won't sell it. It's not a subject with a pound sign. It's an object that connects me to him.

But everything has a price. A quick look at Ebay tells me that there are a staggering 446,503 memorabilia listings – so maybe everything has a starting bid at least. But the words "it's not for sale" can stop the discussion. To some, everything has a price, maybe the price to be sold on, but if the price is emotional then the currency is now redundant. Emotions can not be salved with cash.

I have reviewed the memorabilia industry and there are numerous websites and auctions that my shirt will not appear on. Auctions feature thousands of items out there. It's a fascinating read of memorabilia, price tags and pop history. I wondered who had them and why they sold them? The higher end items display no personal narrative from the owner, so it looks like they are professional collectors buying and selling the history of music – for personal gain. If they bought it and then sold it, that's fine, it's their money. If they found or were given the memorabilia by the artist themselves, I wonder what made them sell; financial clout trumping emotional doubt? Storage issues? Or are they not a fan of the artist anymore, or they wish to sell to buy something else more important, just as substantial or emotionally binding? These are no doubt the answers to some of these sales.

The price of memorabilia is fascinating. But how they come up with these figures is anyone's guess. If it's a case of, it was sold at 'X' amount two years ago and we wish to add 'Y' amount as interest, then I can get to grips with that, I understand. But, some seem like a price plucked out of thin air. The prices are beyond belief. It seemed to be more about an investment than respect for the item. In this case investment overshadows meaning.

Would Morrissey's touch add value to these items?

The following musical instruments from stars of rock and pop music saw sensational prices at Bonham's 10th December Entertainment Memorabilia sale...

The piano which was used to compose almost all of ABBA's greatest hits between 1972-1979 sold for £35,000 to an internet bidder. The piano was originally acquired by the group to be used at a small cottage on the island of Viggsö in the Swedish archipelago, which is where the group wrote their songs. It remained in the cottage until 1979, having been used for the composition of most of the major ABBA hits in this period, including: 'Fernando', 'Mamma Mia', 'Dancing Queen', 'I Do, I Do, I Do, I Do, I Do', 'Money, Mone,y Money', 'Take a Chance on Me', 'The Name of the Game', 'Thank You for the Music', 'Voulez-Vous', 'I Have a Dream', 'Does Your Mother Know' and 'Chiquitita'.

Two guitars (one smashed and mounted on a display) played by The Who in their 1989 25th anniversary tour sold for more than three times the top estimate, achieving £52,500

A rare Led Zeppelin concert poster soared above estimate to achieve £10,625.

Ringo Starr may not have been the best drummer in the Beatles, but he clearly knew a thing or two about cars. A 1964 Vega II Coupé made by the short-lived French luxury carmaker Facel sadly had to be exchanged in 1968 when the drummer was looking to settle down. It sold for £337,500 in December 2013.

A wooden spoon signed by John and Yoko and handed out at a film night they were hosting at the London ICA in 1969 is up for auction at Christie's. This scribbled on perfunctory kitchen utensil is expected to fetch between £800 and £1,200.

A complete set of Monkee's Monthlies. Issues 1 to 32, dated February 1967 to September 1969. The books are full of information, pictures, interviews, song lyrics and much more. Each issue measures 15cm x 21cm (6 inches x 8.25 inches). The condition of the issues is as follows: twelve copies have the owner's name on the reverse cover, one has the owner's name on the front cover, one has a 8cm (3 inch) line written in pen on the front cover and one is slightly scuffed on the front cover otherwise ten of the copies are in very good condition, seventeen are in very good plus condition and five are excellent. £300.00

Eric Clapton Roger Forrester 1981 Tour Itinerary. A 34 page band itinerary for Eric Clapton's 1981 North American tour. Includes details of the concert venues, hotels, flights and travel for the tour. The 34 single sides pages are gripped together and has a Roger Forrester compliment slip stapled to the front page. Roger has also written Roger on the front in a blue pen. Price: £50.00

U2 signed photo – Bono & The Edge autograph signed on a 10" x 8" U2 colour photograph. £39.99

One of the first Ed Sheeran items to come to public auction, a 'Green T' Fender Stratocaster, sold for double top estimate, achieving £12,500.

Are these items of emotional significance or investments? I'll let you decide. Either way the buyers of some are purchasing a unique piece of rock history.

BRITISH MUSIC EXPERIENCE

Memorabilia is big business. Stadium filling rock dogs The Rolling Stones, or the inspirational and sadly missed David Bowie are among the stars who have loaned memorabilia to the British Music Experience that is opened in Summer 2016 – in my home City of Liverpool. It is an exhibition dedicated to 60 years of British pop. It used to be housed in the O2 London where it attracted approximately 350,000 visitors a year which may eventually pay for the £9.5m attraction. It covered a staggering 22,000 square feet. Your feet would be square after walking around it...

And returning to my reliable auction calculator - in my view, if they had more of Morrissey's memorabilia, then the 350,000 visitors a year would treble.

The British Music Experience main player was music impresario Harvey Goldsmith - the man who has worked with all the big names in the music biz including Bob Dylan, The Stones, The Who, The Boss and Zeppelin. Goldsmith has clearly called in a few favours as you will find the tassled outfit worn by The Who singer Roger Daltrey at Woodstock, Jagger's Ossie Clark-designed 1970s jumpsuit and the like.

The O2 experience was not just about looking at famous rock star clothes and guitars. The emphasis was on the interactive experience too with step by step videos at the Gibson Interactive Studio. You can play acoustic/electric guitars alongside well known British artists like KT Tunstall, Amy Macdonald and The Magic Numbers (if you really want to).

And to top it all, there's a full-blown five minute concert to finish, with acts like The Beatles, The Pistols and

Oasis projected around the room for the finale. Morrissey not included? One day perhaps, one day…

Overall, there are approximately 100 artists donating about £5m worth of memorabilia to the display. And according to the promoter, the UK was lacking a venue that "reflects the rich history of fantastic talent that we have spawned continuously that has conquered the world", he said. Well said sir. So Beatleville seemed an obvious choice… The exhibition has now moved to Liverpool, where it will be situated less than a mile away from Mathew St – where four lads began shaking the world and a street began to be as famous as the band.

This area of Liverpool celebrates memorabilia and the brand of a band. From John Lennon's statue, to photographs on walls of public houses that show the Beatles drinking in the local pubs, such as The Grapes on Mathew Street. There is also a hotel named after the Beatles 1964 single and album 'A Hard Day's Night'. And approximately one and a half miles away floating in the Albert Dock is the Yellow Submarine hotel, a stone's throw away, if you can throw quite far, from the statue of Billy Fury, the Liverpool born singer I have adored, for different reasons to Morrissey. Other memorabilia to mention; I have at home a Billy Fury album, signed by Billy's Mum – Jean. She is sweet and polite – a truly wonderful woman.

Furthermore; in Spring 2016, BBC Four opened the door and for a peek at the memorabilia as it launched a new four-part series; The People's History Of Pop. It was an exciting new perspective on the music history for BBC Four; telling the story of popular music through the eyes and ears of the fans and musicians who were there, giving voice to those who were so happy to talk about their precious personal music memorabilia. This series will plot the path of music from as far back as 1950 to the noughties through starry eyed fans. The fan and memorabilia now makes the grade.

It is a series in affiliation with Historypin – which is the user-generated digital archive of historical artefacts. Music fans are asked to upload photos or videos of rock and pop music memorabilia. Leaving performances and artefacts with individual stories attached for all to see.

The items they displayed included photos, badges, ticket stubs, fan club materials, programmes, annuals, diary entries, band recordings, wrist bands and rare footage, which shaped and defined the series. Contributors were also asked to be filmed with their rare material.

The series begins with 1956, the 60th anniversary year; a year of skiffle and rock 'n' roll and a year when the raunchy love affair with British pop music began. The musical journey series will stop at iconic destinations including The TV series 'Ready, Steady, Go', The Beatles final gig in 1966, Northern Soul in Wigan, the Sex Pistols' first gig at Central St Martins' in 1975, the 100 Club's Punk Festival in 1976. Then onto the 80s and the New Romantics at Birmingham's Rum Runner nightclub, Factory Records, through to 1996 and Blur vs Oasis. And let's be honest, I'm hoping to see lots of fans with lots of Pieces of Morrissey.

Currently Morrissey memorabilia on the People History of Pop site, include; The Smiths at Kilburn bootleg and ticket. Tickets stubs for Hop Farm 2011, stubs from The Smiths, Edgbaston, Morrissey's 1991 Victoria Hall Concert, Morrissey fanzines from the 1990's, Morrissey Scrapbooks, Morrissey postcards and posters and a newspaper clipping from The Evening Sentinel (Staffordshire) featuring Morrissey's October 1991 gig at The Victoria Hall, Hanley. All treasured Pieces of Morrissey. Oh and my Morrissey shirt!

I feel this has huge potential; there are lots of

documentaries out there, in there, or over there that celebrate pop and rock artists. But this, I feel, is screaming out as the story of our musical history from another point of view - that of the fans for whom this all means so much.

Could it be seen as a new kind of social experiment, a new perspective on music and its social history? 'I dunno' but, either way, memorabilia is coming to your TV. So, turn off Bob's Full House and enjoy it. I know I will.

And I do hope it puts other music shows to shame that ignore history or give respect to the audience. Such as X Factor. And I do dream it reduces Simon Cowell into giving up whatever he does. Pretty sure my prayers will not be answered on this one. X Factor is for another debate, another book but Simon Cowell's deserves a mention. As BBC4 discusses the history of pop through the eyes of the history makers, X Factor chugs along spraying out manure for the mundane. No more comments about X Factor, but I just had to mention something – it would be rude not to. Then again, let's all be rude – no mention of it again.

Overall the fan and the memorabilia make the grade. The fan now has a voice to discuss their treasured items.

WHY DO I COME HERE ?

One day, early afternoon, when pondering what to do with myself, I made myself the 70th cup of tea of the day. I stopped and stared at my Morrissey shirt, his shirt. The usual 4000 questions fired out, they pinned themselves to the left, right and centre of the brain. I asked myself, why do I behave like this? How can memorabilia end up embracing your life.

Paul Fraser collectibles has a small inkling into this, according to the survey on their website there are some results from a brief survey about the motivations behind collecting and what motivations we are aware of? The collectors emailed their subscribers to find out why they collected and found:

6.7% purchase collectibles solely as an investment

18.0% purchase collectibles solely for the pleasure of ownership

69.3% purchase collectibles for a combination of investment purposes and pleasure of ownership

All good reasons and an insight into collecting and I'm in the pleasure of ownership category – are you?

1980'ZZZZZZZZZZZZZ

I remember the time I found Morrissey. It was the moment a shoddy decade suddenly woke up.

It was the late 1980's and a simple movement moved me forever. Simply pressing 'play' on a cassette player stopped me in my tracks. For those not plotted or jotted around the earth in 1980's – trust me, it was bleak, dank and frustrating.

In Liverpool the 1980's were a time of turmoil, unrest and upheaval. Unemployment and economic unpredictability led to widespread uneasiness and anxiety. Playing football on the streets, you could sense the unrest, playing football in the park, you could sense the unrest and playing football amongst burnt out cars – the unrest was visible.

Public resistance and signs of widespread disquiet escalated to the point of the Toxteth riots of 1981. Margaret Thatcher and her single handed campaign to ruin the North of England was in full motion. There was panic in the streets alright. And enough panic for the city of Liverpool to want away from its own country.

For centuries Liverpool and its workers had fed the South via one of the world's biggest ports. But now, following industrial decline, the South just fed themselves. Liverpool didn't fit in or conform to Thatcher's vision of England. Liverpudlians felt closer to Glaswegians and Dubliners than to the people of London. A shared Irish heritage overriding national boundaries. Those in London didn't care. No one cared – we felt like outsiders, I think we still do.

Liverpool elected its first Labour council in 1983 and

they promised to stand up for what they saw as unjust cuts under the Thatcher government. Militant Supporters were elected to major positions within the Labour Party and in 1983 Labour won the city council elections on a radical socialist manifesto. 1983 was the year Margaret Thatcher won her second general election.

"1983 – Give me the gun ….a job half done – isn't done"

The Labour manifesto led to the cancellation of 1200 redundancies planned by the previous administration. They froze council rents and launched a house-building programme targeting the deprived and needy areas of Liverpool. Slums were torn down, new leisure centres and nurseries built and many apprenticeships created but there was a problem.

Money changes everything, especially when you don't have any. The council did not have the cash. They asked the Government for cash to protect the people of Liverpool and were confident of the answer being yes. Government officials arrived in Liverpool, including the secretary of state for environment. The officials were shocked at standards of living and awarded the council £20million for improvements.

The following year, they asked for more and received a huge crack on the head for asking. No – no more money.

So, alongside other councils campaigning against cuts–in order to balance the books, the council borrowed £100m from foreign banks, but one by one – the other councils left Liverpool to its own devices. The outsider was born.

Politics was everywhere; pubs, clubs, streets, bus stops, bedrooms, living rooms, kitchens and car parks. In the North, South, East and West of Liverpool. We all had a say, we all wanted the world to listen.

Not all agreed with Liverpool Council and in October 1985, thousands gathered at the City's Pier Head for a Liverpool against militant demonstration and even recorded an anti-militant record – rubbish, but well meant. Talking of rubbish, Margaret Thatcher was concerned the city was going bankrupt and wished for Commisioners to run the city. But the City didn't want Thatcher or her concern. They wanted the tools to run a city without Thatcher and London.

And in a last ditch attempt to force the Government to compromise, the council issued 31,000 council workers with redundancy notices. A tactic we were told. No one would lose their jobs said the deputy leader of the council. It was a tactic to buy time and to meet legal obligations. But, it was a tactic Labour Leader Neil Kinnock wasn't happy with. He was furious. And stated that it was infantile and people were petrified with the possibility of losing jobs. This attempt to impress a Government added more worry to people who are already bruised and battered. It wasn't the time for games.

Kinnock made the redundancy notices his centrepiece of his attack on the Militant tendency at the Labour Party conference in 1985. And just after, the party started an eradication of Liverpool militants and the District Auditor banned the Liverpool Labour councillors from public office for five years. What Liverpool wanted was the tools to sort our own problems, many still do, others still don't.

The people of Liverpool were strong in the face of this upheaval, and glimpses of light can be found in dark times. We all seemed to be the outsider, but all outsiders together bring unity and a stern warning to others – take us on at your peril.

What was sad, was that the city has so much to offer. The city was being thrashed and beaten daily by those who didn't care. But this city still has history and heritage – they couldn't take that away from us. For instance; The city of Liverpool was created in 1207 when King John granted a Royal Charter which was written in Latin. Liverpool was once the "Second City of Empire", eclipsing even London for commerce at times. Liverpool's Walker Art Gallery is the national gallery of the North and houses one of the best collections of European art outside London. Liverpool has the largest collection of Grade II-listed buildings outside London. The city has 2,500 listed buildings and 250 public monuments. Liverpool's Anglican Cathedral is the largest cathedral in Britain and the fifth largest in the world. It was designed by Giles Gilbert Scott in 1904. The city has a second cathedral – the Metropolitan Cathedral, which was designed by Frederick Gibberd after the Second World War. Liverpool holds the Guinness Book of Records title for being the Capital of pop. More artists with a Liverpool origin have had a number one hit than from any other location. And of course Liverpudlian legends The Beatles changed the face of popular music.

And finally, cuisine of the scouse is known around the world! It's called 'Scouse' which is pretty much straight to the point. Scouse is a type of stew. It was eaten by Liverpudlians living in poverty before the 1900s. Ingredients include lamb or beef, cabbage, carrot, potatoes and onion.

Lamb or beef? There's always a fly in the ointment.

Overall, the 1980s was bleak for many. Not just in Liverpool, but for many around the country. It was the decade of chunky mobiles and chunky yuppies holding them. 1980's music saw the rise of rap and hip hop music, with American influences powerful once again in the form of such groups as; Run DMC and Grandmaster Flash and the Furious Five. It was the 1980's. I was furious myself.

It saw the rise and fall of New Romantics; Adam and

the Ants dressing like highway men, Boy George and his club of culture, Michael Jackson and his club in the back garden and Paul Hardcastle being played in all the clubs. The ego club called Band Aid and the chuckle brothers club - Matt And Luke Goss as Bros which equals – club dross.

We all had new neighbours with Kylie and Jason and we were all unsure which one was which. We also had many rock bands with the Division 2 footballer's haircut. Bleached blonde hair the length of a snooker table with ripped jeans and pretty much nothing to say or offer. Tape decks and personal CD players came out and soon went back in again. As something would break. Usually the cassette ribbon would wrap itself around the tape deck. It seemed to act like a noose for the tape deck that had decided to give up its one role in life, to actually work.

Add all this to watching; Argentina invading the Falklands Islands and then Britain going to war, led by Mrs Foghorn and the permanent headache -Margaret Thatcher. And also, dumped on us all whether you wanted it or not was the "whoop de whoop" events of Charles marrying Diana and Andrew, whoever he is, - marrying Sarah Ferguson.

There was nothing but orgasmic delight in the papers, there was orgasmic joy on the TV news, and orgasmic pleasure heard on the radio. Is there anything worse than a Royal Correspondent? But, there was displeasure among the people I knew.

These pantomime events for a period of time saw jingoistic Britain wanting the country to applaud when their people could barely eat. I sat in amazement as the crowds gathered for the weddings. Naïve folk sat out for 3 days under a Union Jack tent with a union Jack flask, with a face full of union jack face paint to watch people be married together in unity – that unity is based on not caring about what goes on in the real world.

I grew up amongst all of this. And growing up; in a savage social and political climate seemed wrong. Knowing so much, so young, seemed wrong. Knowing so much inequality and knowing no one really cares, seemed wrong. Knowing people didn't really like each other was wrong. Watching people struggle – seemed wrong. Knowing Governments and the Royal Family won't help – is wrong, but there is nothing new there. I knew this is the case by the time we reached the 1980s and I was born in 1972. It was silent and grey, school was grey, and society was grey. It was a precarious time full of cautionary tales of what to do and what not to do. It was full of crap promises and lies. But it was life. And the only life I knew.

School had conned me. Since I left school, I've educated myself. Back then, teachers were afraid of the pupils and teachers were afraid to be inspirational. I was lucky if they turned up for the day. 'Life is a serious business Sir'

But, it wasn't all bad – family and friends delightfully shone and my cat and dog brought the tranquility and peace I needed. A true friendship was born as the animals looked at me for love, food and an alliance. I didn't need words from them, trust and commitment was on display everyday. Their eyes and my eyes spelt out friendship. Two animals I still cry for whenever I think of them. They were part of me, I was in the heart of them.

My neighbours and their neighbours all remained a unit and community was part of the spirit I experienced around me. TV etched some fun and some not so fun. Brookside was great! I loved it. It was located near my old school and I'd wander down to the close and peek in. I also spotted the odd actor or actress in between takes. I just stared in hope they would ask me to join them. And I was hoping we could sell up and move there but dreams have a knack of not coming true.

For the football mad boy, I was also selected to be a ballboy at Everton F.C. – Goodison Park. A day to treasure. Well it was until just before half time, I was hit in the head, not by the ball, not from a wayward shot, – but, by a cheese, ham and onion sandwich, thrown by a Norwich fan. The sandwich didn't even look appealing, Delia wouldn't be happy. It certified my route to vegetarianism. Everton won quite a bit in the 1980s – to my pleasure. But on this day, Everton lost and it rained.

But what really sparkled, on a daily basis, was the haven in a box. The family collection of vinyl records and a box of tapes my Dad found in a hedge as he walked home from nights. Many cassettes and many questions; how did they end up in a bag, on a hedge? No answers were needed just thank you Mr Hedge. Either way, I placed the vinyl and the tape decks on display in front of me. I was there staring at them before school and after school. This was the future, cos the present was pretty crap.

I remember the records rotating, gyrating and mesmerising on the turntable – the artist and its spirit spinning and spelling out beautiful concepts and thoughts. Playing a record moved me. The record box consisted of all the big players of 60'and 70s pop stars; records included Dylan, The Beatles and The Everly Brothers.

But, there was only a few artists I took seriously. There were only a few I wanted to sing along to, these artists didn't let me down. I wanted to see them after a good day, or a bad day at school. I only wanted to spend my teatime with them. Arriving home, I'd say 'hello', leaving home, I'd say 'goodbye' and of an evening - I'd say 'goodnight'. And in the winter I'd even wrap them up to keep them warm.

Eventually, I decided to have a series of duets with

the artists who pleased me most; Billy Fury, Elvis Presley and The Everly Brothers. They spoke to me as I shuffled across my bedroom, my school tie as the microphone and microphone lead. The bed was the amp, the posters my audience – a concert for one in my own home. I even staged a few encores. And for effect I'd appear from behind the wardrobe door.

All of them were special artists, but deep down, I still wanted more. And I looked everywhere for it, all around me. I tried everywhere. Switching on the radio brought me more music, but also brought me much confusion. Was it real or pantomime pop? Or was life pantomime and was pop real life?

I was growing up, I was shy, I was vulnerable. I was scared of the future, I was scared of the present. I was scared of the day. I was scared of the night. I was scared of the way I looked, the clothes I wore and the things I said. I was scared of school and its offer of nothingness. I was scared of working life as work seemed delicate and could easily be withdrawn. People seemed to be a big bag of nerves. I wanted a hand on my shoulder. I wanted defiance and I wanted my vulnerability to be society's problem, not mine. I wanted someone to say something to me, about me, from someone who knew me. Teachers hadn't bothered and family didn't understand but I didn't ask them either. They had their own problems.

Yet none of the above seemed to matter when I pressed play on that afternoon in the late 1980's. Because colour, at last, came into my world. Sunglasses were needed. This was bright, this was perfect. This moment was the answer to a question I had not yet devised. As the tape deck button cemented into position the ears pricked and the eyebrows raised and the heart at last, had found a another heart within.

"ASK"

Shyness is nice, and
Shyness can stop you
From doing all the things in life
You'd like to

Shyness is nice, and
Shyness can stop you
From doing all the things in life
You'd like to

So, if there's something you'd like to try
If there's something you'd like to try
ASK ME - I WON'T SAY "NO" - HOW COULD I?

Coyness is nice, and
Coyness can stop you
From saying all the things in
Life you'd like to

So, if there's something you'd like to try
If there's something you'd like to try
ASK ME - I WON'T SAY "NO" - HOW COULD I?

Spending warm Summer days indoors
Writing frightening verse
To a buck-toothed girl in Luxembourg

ASK ME, ASK ME, ASK ME
ASK ME, ASK ME, ASK ME

Because if it's not Love
Then it's the Bomb, the Bomb, the Bomb, the Bomb, the Bomb,
the Bomb, the Bomb

That will bring us together

Nature is a language - can't you read?
Nature is a language - can't you read?

SO...ASK ME, ASK ME, ASK ME
ASK ME, ASK ME, ASK ME

Because if it's not Love
Then it's the Bomb, the Bomb, the Bomb, the Bomb, the Bomb,
the Bomb, the Bomb
That will bring us together

If it's not Love
Then it's the Bomb
Then it's the Bomb
That will bring us together

SO...ASK ME, ASK ME, ASK ME
ASK ME, ASK ME, ASK ME

Shyness? Coyness? Buck-toothed girl in Luxembourg? How? What? Why? This is... ugh, erm... help! Calm down! Sit down Matthew, play it again, Matthew, play it again...

Life was now beginning to feel complete. It was adolescent bashfulness - for the bashful adolescent. The most perfect pop painting was now being painted before me. The hero was born. At last I am born. The box of records was now destitute and the albums by The Smiths and Morrissey had to be explored and adored. And I did and I still do. And here I am 30 years later, staring at Morrissey's shirt with boxes full of records by The Smiths and Morrissey.

But, then, why do I stand and stare at the shirt and why do I wish for more memorabilia? Why do I wish for the trousers to go with the shirt? The shoes to go with the trousers? Why do I put it on display? And why do I spend days thinking of adding something special to my collection. Is it normal behaviour? If not, what is normal? Am I asking too many questions? I see it as normal, but many don't. But these behaviours are unique to me and the fans express similar behaviours. As a whole, to me, it's just all a bit lovely.

In terms of fandom and obsession, many have studied and tried to comment on behaviours. For this project, I have read many articles and books and even spoken to a qualified psychologist on the behaviours of fandom. I don't really know why, or what I expected to find out. I was just intrigued the way fans can change overnight under the influence of an artist.

Connection is a wonderful and powerful thing. I honestly don't know what I would have done without it. Something would not have been right, something would not have been complete. How Morrissey interprets this world is part of the way I think – without this, my thoughts would have been two thirds rhubarb and one part custard.

Poking my nose into fandom and obsession, I read an article written about idolatry and its "salient role" during adolescence. It set the scene of a typical concert; the house lights dimmed and the curtains drew open. The artist made his way to centre stage, as a sea of fans overcome with excitement, emotion and genuine adoration, celebrate with a cacophony of shrieks and roars – there were screams and tears, emotions and adulation at the forefront of the night. The artist in question was interrupted by marriage proposals and love letters tossed from the crowd. Pandemonium breaks out as he launches into his repertoire of hits

The artist in question wasn't Morrissey but Franz Liszt at the Italian Opera House in Berlin in 1842. The 19th century Hungarian piano virtuoso has two claims to fame; he was the first 'pop star' and the first to have 'mania' added as a suffix to his tongue twisting name. Since Liszt, there have been many artists just like him, to create that storm of adulation; Sinatra, Presley, The Beatles, all the way up to the pop artist formally known as a pop artist 'Beiber'.

All are capable of capturing imaginations, emotions and at times, breaking hearts. But although they create a storm of adulation, their lyrical content and presence, well, it just isn't Morrissey is it? But, am I paying the price for devotion?

IS THERE A PRICE TO PAY?

Dr Alan Ravitz, might, or might not know. Dr Ravitz, Child and adolescent psychiatrist at the Child Mind Institute in New York City, says

"As kids individualize themselves from their parents, which is a natural part of development and growing up, they try to establish psychological and emotional independence. No matter the culture, they need somebody to look to, aside from their parents, for guidance and a model for becoming an adult. In our culture, this is often a sports figure, an actor, or a pop star."

So, it was natural, normal and kind. It happened for a reason. I was searching, I did need it and I'm glad I found it. Parents can guide with a natural parental bias and my teachers guided with weapons of a mass chalk dusters and fists. But, I wanted the voice of another. Someone established in the world and someone who made sense of this world for me. And I found it.

However, I am unsure if all people need somebody to look to, as many people have expressed to me, they don't necessarily find a hero or icon. Not because parents or teachers filled the gap, but they just didn't find anyone they could connect with. Many have also expressed a sadness they didn't find an icon – sadly no-one suited. But, have faith. I'll send them 'Meat is Murder' by next Monday.

Dr. Ravitz says that children have "rich" fantasy lives, and when fantasy is coupled with the drive for independence, the end result of seemingly irrational adoration is predictable. "Adults may find it puzzling, even irritating, but it's not trivial," he explains. "We call it 'child's play,' but it's actually part of the work necessary for healthy development."

For me, it can't be healthy if you like the wrong artist! Again my bias is here in black and white as my life continues in grey and grey. Firstly, I'm not too sure what a 'rich' fantasy life is. My fantasy life was just as poor as real life. As a football mad; football kit wearing, boot wearing whipper-snapper, I wanted to play football for Everton. I realised I wasn't good enough and after the cheese and ham ball boy attack, I wasn't brave enough. They didn't even move the scattered cheese and dead flesh sandwich off the grass. Big goalkeeper Neville Southall was tempted for a snack though, but those gloves would have been the big stumbling block, no chance of picking up grated cheese with those gloves on Nev, or is it Neville?

After finding music, I then wanted to mount the stage and sing, but I can't sing, well I think I can, everyone else thinks I have problems with the actual singing part. I even wrote a song at school – untitled - it started with;

"The future must be better than the past

Cos up to now it's been f★★★★★n last"

And there lies the fact I cannot write songs (or books I hear you say). I then wanted to basically do something away from the mundane. Anything really. But this was fantasy and it didn't happen either. Overall, I'm unsure what people would class as rich fantasy? Flying to the moon on a horse, water-skiing through Venice, having a house made of jammy dodgers. Whatever it is – I didn't have it and never will.

I also note the comments "and when fantasy is coupled with the drive for independence, the end result of seemingly irrational adoration is predictable" I think everyone drives for some kind of independence but, irrational adoration is predictable. What is irrational about adoration? Maybe we just adore, idolize, love, keep in high regard etcetera because the artist is worthy to be adored, idolized, loved and kept in high regard. The finest art can bring the world to a standstill. Irrational and predictable could be words used to describe the theory above. But anyway, I didn't have the rich fantasy in the first place.

"Adults may find it puzzling, even irritating, but it's not trivial," he explains. "We call it 'child's play,' but it's actually part of the work necessary for healthy development."

The adults I know have found it puzzling, but many say, " in my day, I was obsessed with such and such" or " I'd understand if it was such and such" or "no, I never had a hero so I don't understand how you can be obsessed". No-one has ever called it child's play if they have said something similar, then, there has always been a smirk or laugh to accompany the comment.

As for healthy development, well it certainly helped me, I'm just unhealthy full stop. But I understand, it's not trivial, it can aid you as a person and make you stand tall and believe in yourself, it can change your life – it did mine.

Many studies have set out to understand why adolescents are prone to idolatry. One study in particular; the Adolescent Idolization of Pop Singers: Causes, Expressions, and Reliance concluded that "idolization is, in fact, a required element of youth culture". The study examines the phenomenon of adolescents and the idolization of the pop singer.

First thing wrong with this, all pop singers are different. They say different things and mean different things to fans. Fans I think want different things; music, dance, lyrics, voice, interviews , live experience can be mixed around in order of priority or grouped together, or ignored. Artists have different styles concepts and thoughts. Surely, artists mean something for different reasons; Bono would mean something different to those who like Kajagoogoo, Chris Martin would mean something different to those who like Kajagoogoo. And Kajagoogoo would mean something different to those who like a Chris Martin and Bono. But the point is not lost. Not all artists are the same. The artist is different, I think the study should be the fan against the artist. Therefore not all pop obsessions are the same.

Morrissey's lyrics are tender, humorous, insightful, real, and believable. This is a major connection. And Oasis fans may feel lyrics are not as important to them as the rock 'n' roll blast of music or the image of the Gallagher brothers that brilliantly blasted them into the 1990's (I maybe wrong but it's what I've been told).

Dylan fans talk of the greatest storyteller of all time, I should now, my Dad and Uncle Kevin talk forever about Bob Dylan. (My uncle Kevin talks forever full stop) but the theme is storytelling. A storytelling theme certainly not discussed when Michael Jackson fans try to moonwalk in high pitched short trousers, wearing white socks and sparkly gloves.

The study saw males and females compared with regard to the intensity of idolization, ages ranging from 10–11, 13–14, and 16–17 were all compared; with behavioural symptoms and expressions and causes for selecting the idol. Results indicated that girls idolise more than boys. And the phenomenon of idolisation, expressed by those worshipping and modelling is strongest in the youngest age group and certainly decreases with age. Errr, I'm 43 and it's not slowing down.

I feel idolisation of pop stars has inimitable characteristics for adolescents. It can provide a basis for self-expression, or the creation of self-identity and the attainment of independence. As mentioned previously, I feel my identity changed as the obsession rolled on. Matthew 'he's a

Morrissey fan' - seems to be my surname.

COMMON? YES.
HARMLESS? PERHAPS NOT

Dr. Lin Fang, an assistant professor in the faculty of Social Work at the University of Toronto, believes idolatry plays a "salient role" during adolescence and warns parents of adolescent children about its darker side – not just from popstars but from all celebrities. Well, we all know there are some celebrities that have shown their darker side, one in particular called James on the television promised to fix things - when they weren't broken.

"Research shows that girls who strongly idolize celebrities tend to buy into other aspects of commercial culture and may become overly materialistic," she says. "The pressure coming from celebrities with perfect bodies may lead to an unrealistic body image and possibly nurture eating disorders, which can consume a child's life." This, sadly, is a huge concern. And I feel the fault of the depressing celebrity culture we live in.

Dr Lin Fang also warns "Idolizing and worshipping pop stars may also consume a child's life to the point where they neglect real-life relationships and isolate themselves from friends." I think the word may is relevant here. It can consume a life, but isolating from friends, if anything, it can also make friends. The MozArmy is testament to that. At each gig or at the MozArmy meet in Manchester's Star and Garter – you find a room full of wonderful souls with one common sovereign – Morrissey. I'm sure other artists have a similar fan base, with similar friendships, it just can't be the same, because, as mentioned, not all artists are the same. Other artists have fans and their friendships may be well received and it's a tribute to them – I'll never knock that but it has something missing. It doesn't include the reason for our friendships Morrissey.

Dr Lin continues, "the entertainment pages of newspapers and websites are often filled with stories about celebrities who are in trouble with the law. Children may think it is acceptable to get drunk and black out, drink and drive, or engage in violent behaviour."

Well, if any statement ever sums up what Morrissey doesn't do, it's the above. Many people get drunk, not just celebs, I do and I am now, but, for us Morrissey fans, it's almost as if Morrissey doesn't exist anywhere. He is not splattered across the rag and bone media. He is very selective and this is largely unique amongst the popstar world. I really respect that, I feel it's one of the main attractions to Morrissey. He doesn't need the media, but the media need him. He is now carefree. They have hurt him – but will not kill him. They are now the quarry.

Morrissey gets into trouble by just opening his mouth. His words, full of social justice, are routinely condemned by individuals who are full of pomposity and credulous beliefs. It is a shame, as it seems it is okay for others to speak, but Morrissey isn't allowed. It is shocking snootiness and so sad to see. He has a right to speak, unfortunately, others who don't like his beliefs can aim, shoot and fire before the Vinyl has hit the shelf or in fact, even, before the new release has actually been planned for release.

They Need Advice!

Dr Ravitz had practical advice for parents "each case is different" and at last we have landed on planet common sense, I just wish they realised artists are different and the reasons we like artists can be for different reasons.

According to Dr. Ravitz "it's important for parents to remember that the idolization of celebrities, especially pop stars, is to be expected" I feel this takes away something from the artist. It shouldn't just be expected. For me, it's expected if they display a huge amount of talent with intellect, flair and flowers in their back pockets – it's expected. But, not so much if you are Coldplay, sorry, low dig I know. The Doctor continues, "these sorts of crushes are necessary for, and directed by, a young person's development," he says. "By definition, they have nothing to do with parents—they are about getting away from parents. So don't encourage, do keep track, and be prepared to intervene if your child has a major change in mood or behaviour."

All cases are different. I don't feel finding a hero is one way of dismissing your parents. Art can attack you when you aren't expecting it. It can take you on a different direction or a different path and there is nothing to be scared of when it does. Personally I didn't have to get away from parents, I just did. If anything, my parents were happy that I had found a world away from them – it gave them a breather. I had found something charming that got under my skin and made me feel something. At last I was blooming, at last I was captivated and at last I felt victorious. There was a major change in my behaviour, but nothing (I feel) negative just the sheer delight that I had found a triumphant interest.

My parents didn't intervene, they didn't need to. Although, on one occasion, in the early 1990's my Mum did ask - why did I buy clear lens, NHS style glasses for £45? I replied something on the lines of a grunt, a huff and a puff, and how that was cheap to look like one of Morrissey's disciples. To me they added the final touch. The quiff was perfected with Levi jeans with turn-ups ironed to perfection. And as for the suit jacket, although tailored and smart, it looked second hand, because it was.

I remember the first time I wore the glasses. It was cold and the sun was going down. After a long day at work, I headed home from Liverpool City Centre. I was tired and bored but, looking forward to my room – with my things – in my world. I stepped off the bus and I was very content, I was nearly home. I dodged the people doing people things; the shop owners getting ready to shut the shop they own and the postman crouching down, emptying the postbox on his last pick up of the day. The sun shone brightly, but it highlighted a smudge on my glasses and the lens. It made the walk home slightly wobbly and irritating. So, I stopped and took them off. I dug out the cloth from my pocket and began to clean the lens with the cloth.

And then, from just outside the nearest shop, I heard, a scouse quizmaster ask the first question; "eh mate, penny for the guy Elvis?" I looked down at my glasses and smirked. If I had kept the glasses on would he have asked say Penny for the guy Morrissey? I smirked and gave him £2. The quizmaster quizzed again and asked the second question of the day. Two pound really, are you sure mate? Yes, that's for calling me Elvis. Calling me Morrissey would have earned you a fiver. The quizmaster looked confused, but still eating his bag of Wotsits that seemed to be located around his face, he asked, "who is he like?" "No time to answer that question son, have a nice night with your guy and the pennies and pounds you make, invest them wisely." "Will do mate". I heard him shuffle away and inform his friends of the £2.

At that point I realised, there was no 'guy', it was his friend, covered up in a thousand coats with half a burst and ripped football over his face. And amazingly he jumped up and asked his friend for a share of the coinage. I still have the glasses, they are broken but they are still here. But, one arm has caused harm by snapping and leaving the glasses seeking counselling for a broken heart.

Anyway, back to the point; what would parents say

anyway? I could understand if financial problems occurred or the nature of the obsession was dangerous. Religious or political missions that are open to problems; with unease, nervousness and concern. I won't list any – feel free to fill in the gaps.

And I understand and agree with Dr. Ravitz comments. "I can say that if a young person becomes seriously despondent over a pop crush, she can sustain emotional damage. But if a child or teen becomes depressed, tries to hurt herself, or even tries to kill herself over a pop star, it's likely because there is an underlying emotional problem that has more to do with genetics or environment than with, say, Justin Bieber," he adds. Agreed Dr Ravitz, I just hope all find the help they need. I really do.

Dr Ravitz comments on teenage, adolescent, day-to-day fandom, and youthful obsession over an artist or a band or a celeb in the overblown celeb world. Dr Ravitz states, "Intervening can be as simple as sitting down with your child and showing a genuine interest in the artists and music they like. Not only will this process provide a parent with the opportunity to get to know their child a little better, it may even strengthen a much needed bond at such a pivotal time in their child's life."

For my circumstances, no intervention was required but, if anything I invited my folks into my world. I've asked them many times, "Mum, Dad listen to this Morrissey song", "watch this Morrissey video", "read this Morrissey lyric" to the point they had to – just to shut me up. And after many years of suggesting this song and that song I succeeded. Although I didn't manage to get them to a concert, I managed to take them along to see the excellent 'Morrissey 25' – at Liverpool FACT. A delightful night; the concert received a standing ovation at the end. Just like the real thing.

Overall, it was an insight and I enjoyed giving them a peek into my world – but they had to leave my world early, no stay behinds, I think they prefer their world! They aren't Morrissey fans by any stretch of the imagination but they enjoy some of the music and I think they have a real soft spot for Him.

WHAT ARE YOU DREAMING ABOUT ?

For the music fan, fandom and obsession is based on the connection with the artist. It's a full blown commitment that leads to full dedication on a sparkly diamond devoted path. You are joined together – the soul of the artist and the fan joined in matrimony. No wedding rings needed. It's just beautiful, powerful and emotional. Comrades for life.

I have friends who like Morrissey and friends who are obsessed with other artists. And while we all obsess over our heroes, I believe we know our place in the realms of the artist/fan connection. I really wanted Morrissey to know my name, just for him to say once 'Matthew Jacobson'. I've dreamt of it because anything else may be too difficult to comprehend. One more sentence may send me into a mound of sentimental skin and bones puree. I hope it happens (not the puree aspect obviously) but just for that moment. Many fans feel the same. The feedback I received was honest and open. Fans really want to meet Morrissey but many respect his privacy. They would not like to intrude. Just one day they hope to cross his path and there it is – a quick chat, a hello and an autograph and the world is a safer place.

I have dreamt of the song with my name in. Or jumping on stage for the on-stage handshake and his recognition. Or the vegetarian meal for two in Los Angeles or Liverpool whichever is easiest. Finished off by a Grey Goose Vodka and an exchange of email addresses for a lifetime of correspondence. But, I know I'm nothing special. So why should it happen to me? I can but dream. I'm not selfish, I want the same for many Morrissey fans.

Other feedback from fans indicated, as they have a talent

for music, their dream was to write a song with him, or to tour with Morrissey and to be part of his band forever. Other fans wanted to be Morrissey's tour manager, personal assistant, window cleaner, driver or even his gardener. But, inadvertently, they all want to be his friend. Which in this world is a sweet aspect amongst the human race.

This obsession of fans and request to be friends with the artist is evident. And friends of mine, who like other groups or artists follow suit with their obsession. They go to nightclubs that play their music. Some wear the leather jackets and the ripped jeans. They proudly wear the badges, the T-shirts, the patches as they launch their hair, which is the length of a Ford Cortina, across the dancefloor. But deep down they wish for the same thing. To be close to the artist.

I understand. They are loyal and dedicated. Their music may not be my cup of tea, but my tea is not their favourite either. They just want to be the best friend on the payroll. But, will that ever work out?

Knock Knock
Who's There?
Talent
Go Away

But these dreams may seem silly to others. Many people, regardless of the artist, will question the sanity of fans. But, for me, in this world – this is not dangerous or extreme behaviour. No harm is meant from the fans who have contacted me. No risk or over-zealous behaviour. They all respect Morrissey and the life he lives.

For me the subversive artist is not allowed to be as visible these days – although they must exist, surely? Reality television and pop show factories seem to be killing off the chances for us to ever see a hero again – a real artist rather than the farmyard scraps of mud and manure we see each Saturday night. Yes, all artists are different and fandom and obsession can stem and be born from any artist. But I just feel the artist capable of changing the times isn't welcome anymore. After all, most of the ground-breaking artists of yesteryear were outcasts from the music industry and only gradually accepted before they were later idolized by the money men; The Beatles were knocked back dozens of times before they got a deal and The Sex Pistols were banned from every town in the country at one point. So it's no surprise that money talks.

Is music dead? Am I biased but those with something different to say seem to be compressed, pounded and grounded down and barred from the TV studios of Britain. Maybe I'm just getting old. Then again, I know I am, but, I also know times have changed. Television, social media and the internet have changed the minds of the fan and the individual.

Instant selfie, instant tweet, instant Facebook message or instant Instagram images have changed the interest people pay in artists. People now pay more interest to themselves. Instant fame = instant shame.

The dreams of the Morrissey fans or the long haired lovers from Liverpool, Hartlepool or Pontypool wishing to be a member of the band, a tour manager , a gardener or personal assistant for their hero is harmless, I know. But, it is even more so when you hear the dreams of the future of our country. The new kids on the block want to be a celeb regardless of anything. Household names or criminally insane?

TEACHERS ARE AFRAID THEY WILL HAVE NO PUPILS TO TEACH

In 2009, *The Telegraph* produced reports from researchers into the future plans of the children of our future. There has been an upsurge of change in career aspiration. As traditional careers have lost out in the search for stardom, modern children dream of becoming celebrities where once they aspired to a professional career.

A study, commissioned to mark the launch of new TV series 'Tarrant Lets the Kids Loose' on Sky channel Watch on October 4 revealed: twenty-five years ago, adolescents wished to become bankers, teachers or doctors. But these days, teenage Dads and Mums on estates are hoping to discover fame through, sport, music or acting. Television, although a massive influence, has now broken through as the biggest front runner of influencing children's choice of career.

Over 3,000 parents, with children aged five to 11 were quizzed about their little broods and asked about their child's dreams, hopes, goals, career aims and life's desires. Results are surprising, or these days, maybe not;

12% have the top ambition of becoming a sports star; like Wayne Rooney, Beth Tweddle or Eddie the Eagle.

11% wish to follow in the footsteps of X-Factor star Leona and her bleeding heart and bleeding songs Lewis, as they wish to make it big as a popstar. Interesting it doesn't mention, "as Morrissey, David Bowie, John Lennon, Billy Fury or Elvis Presley". But 'X-Factor star Leona Lewis'. I'm unsure if the survey was designed with a designated box that asked; please enter the name of the artist. I do hope it didn't and this is an assumption. Otherwise, this country is dead. If it is the case, there is a lesson for us all - never underestimate the power of television. Especially when the television is pants.

11% want to be an actor or actress; like Jude Law, Keira Knightley or the blooming Orlando Bloom.

Over 25 years ago, back then, a career in medicine met with 7% approval and today, becoming a doctor remains almost as (un) popular as today's choice - 6% per cent of the scoundrels fancy helping you with your ills and other things.

And again, over the same twenty-five year timescale, by contrast, teaching was the top objective and dream but now, a skimpy 4% fancy the idea of shouting at children until the children hate life.

A quarter of a century ago, a career in banking and stealing public money captivated 9% of the kiddie's hearts. But, I think they realise it can become a career full of public backlash as the sector did not even make the top then amongst today's little rascals. A wise choice.

The emergency services was absent from popularity in the past, but is now the sixth most popular desire with 7% . Good stuff, well done chaps. And it's not all showbiz you know – I don't care what the thespians say, as they did not feature on the wish list at all. Sad Jazz hands required.

Those wishing to join the space race as on the peak with astronaut Tim Peak is up 4% per cent on twenty-five years ago. And the so called success of the likes of Gordon Ramsay and Jamie 'Orrible' Oliver may explain why becoming a chef is a dream of 5% of the youngsters of today. Drummers drumsticks replaced with chef knives and forks – carry on but, no meat though boys, please, please no meat.

And those with a lovely spirit and a glowing tender and spiritual heart, as those little tinkers understand man to be the cruelest animal and come up trumps as 3% of the all-stars wish to be a vet. God bless you all.

Twenty-five years ago, becoming a scientist was the fourth most popular ambition as six per cent dreamt of bubbly tubes and fermented fumes. But now, it doesn't even register with the You Tube children of today. 0 % fancy the white coat and 15 green pens in the pocket

Overall, there was a deep divide between today's sexes with boys dreaming most of becoming a professional footballer (and the wages that go with it) or an astronaut or firefighter. But, girls meanwhile, want to become a pop star, actress or medic.

Psychologist Laverne Antrobus, signalled a caution to children and unrealistic dreams. To sum up she says children are focusing on the exciting aspects of celebrities, but, Wayne Rooney has huge amounts of talent and has spent many years of dedication perfecting his, whatever it is he has. She continues; 'Dreams have to be based on reality. Perhaps they were not encouraged by their own parents. But, they need to give them guidance and manage their expectations by letting them know the hard work ahead required for certain careers'.

In comparison, she said it was unlikely the parents themselves had never wanted to be pop stars or actors. Also, and in comparison; parents did not sit in front of the box as much as the children, sat glued to the TV or reality shows, or the 45,000 channels we have these days. But also, parents may be selective in memories and forget their failed ambitions. They may not remember they too wanted to mount the stage and to sing their life. As many of us do, why don't you – do you want to?

Paul Moreton, head of the channel, said: "Children have such big imaginations and ambitions, but they can't all be celebrities when they grow up can they?" Paul, it looks like they will give it a go. They wish to squeeze their bodies into and onto the box for their moment of fame. It seems the subversive pop star isn't respected anymore but fame and celebrity is. Fame is certainly the name It is well respected, it is adored, it is reality amongst the reality kids of today. I want to cry.

AMBITIONS OF CHILDREN TODAY

1 Sports star 12%
2 Pop star 11%
3 Actor/actress 11%
4 Astronaut 9%
5 Lawyer 9%
6 Emergency services 7%
7 Medicine 6%
8 Chef 5%
9 Teacher 4%
10 Vet 3%

AMBITIONS OF CHILDREN 25 YEARS AGO

1 Teacher 15%
2 Banking/ finance 9%
3 Medicine 7%
4 Scientist 6%
5 Vet 6%
6 Lawyer 6%
7 Sports star 5%
8 Astronaut 4%
9 Beautician/ hairdresser 4%
10 Archaeologist 3%

Modern children dream of becoming celebrities where once they aspired to a professional career. And I hear people say wishing to be in Morrissey's band, or his tour manager, a gardener, or personal assistant to be strange. The above is ensuring the earth is the most confusing planet of all.

BEING OBSESSED WITH...

those who have been obsessed with...
those who have been obsessed with...
& so on.....

This level of fandom and obsession has reached a fascinating fixation. I fill a daily appetite with big slices of dedicated commitment and a nice cup of sincere warmth. And let's be honest, it's nice – it tastes really nice. Morrissey fandom is here to stay and becomes stronger and more invaluable as our lives drag and drag, on, and on and on.

I wonder how Morrissey feels when he greets this fandom - as he walks on stage into a huge wall of excitement, detonated by blasts and explosions of hysteria. Even before the stage, he must have seen the queues to be front rail, or the jostle to be first at the stage door. And as the night unfolds, he can see and hear the plea and desire for a handshake and he can certainly see the frantic uphill scramble to jump on stage for a hug or to come away with an item of clothing.

For me, fandom is understood by Morrissey and he understands the meaning of being a fan. On stage – Morrissey reaches out to the fan, understanding and aware a handshake will help them, or rescue them; a moment to treasure. He often verbally shoves security aside to allow him to be closer to the fans and fans to be closer to him. And this provides a chance for a fan to hug or bear hug him as he sings his life.

And within interviews he is always respectful to his fans and always complimentary. His devotees are loyal and he is forever loyal to his devotees. Morrissey understands fandom, because has been a devotee to his own heroes. Look at Morrissey's feelings and his words on his heroes. What springs to mind – any links - any feelings stirred?

Morrissey on:

James Dean: "for me he is the only person who looked perfect persistently" 'Send me anything Jimmy touched. If he touched a wall, send me a piece of the wallpaper.'

Marc Bolan: Hustled out of a venue in 1986, Morrissey noticed a Bolan poster in the background - "he was looking directly at me and for me it was a very strange mystical moment. It was like he was almost staring at me - it was a shiver down the spine"

Billy Fury: "Billy's singles are totally treasurable - he always had such profound passion"

Patti Smith: "I have never heard or seen anything like Patti Smith previously and I have never heard truth established so sincerely".

Nico: "Minutes later I am walking home and - a wet heap of diffident stoop. I take the stairs at Kings Road where Nico is always waiting for me"

Sparks: "The first five Sparks albums had been constant companions". (Morrissey loved the idolatrous Sparks, he loved Sparks so much so that he is alleged to have stolen even their breakfast sandwiches).

For me, if I could quite easily replace the artists name with Morrissey's name – it's a mirror image of how I feel about him. What about you? I could, if he allows me, use his words to describe him;

"He looks perfect persistently",

"If he touched your door, send me your house and

street!'".

"I've felt his stare in my posters"

"I feel his music is totally treasurable, he always has such profound passion.

"I had never heard or seen anything like Morrissey - he has always been there for me when I returned home "

"His albums / singles etc are constant companions" (But does anyone know where Morrissey has his breakfast?!)

Morrissey understands fandom as he too has waited by a stage door for his heroes and he's also asked his heroes for photos and autographs.

On Bowie; "The first time I saw him, which was at a stage door in Manchester, he was arriving for the sound check, and there was nobody around but me and a few of those scruffy little kids, and he emerged from this car dressed in his absolute glamorous finery with the most enormous women's shoes. And it was very impressive".

The stage door hover and loiter is all part of fandom and the dream to meet your icon. I feel these moments, are romantic, exciting, stimulating and alluring - alluring enough to make you wait for hours looking at a big metal door. Or to stand by the big metal door, looking down a road awaiting a big metal bus to stop by the big metal stage door – for your hero to gracefully step off and wave hello to you and your comrades.

Or it's alluring enough for you, well me, to stand outside the Apollo, in the rain, on a box and a wall , then on a railing to try and glimpse Morrissey step off the tour bus - I didn't see him, but I was there and ready. Yes, of course it's worth the wait; in the cold, in the rain, in the wind or in the snow – and in all four mixed together if you live in the North.

But, at that moment when the artist walks past you, from, or onto the tour bus, your mind quickly takes 1000 pictures and just like you do with a camera film (or if you are younger than myself – a mobile phone!), you pick the best snapshot to remember the moment. It leaves the most perfect Polaroid planted in the mind. It was and maybe your only chance in your lifetime, of dedication – for your artist to recognise you and hopefully recognise your devotion.

I've stood by many stage doors waiting for Morrissey and the Polaroids have been processed and planted into my mind. Images imposed and stapled to the memory office of the brain. I've seen him at stage doors opened in Liverpool, London and Copenhagen to name a few. And I've met the band in Leeds, London and San Jose. As one door opens - I never see it shutting, because as that point the door shuts – a hero is walking by. Lyrics and voice are a wonderful combination and the strength and pull this can have can transform a life once lived. Fandom is a beautiful thing.

The world can be brutal; well it is brutal, harsh, and uncompromising. It's riddled with unbalanced power and unbalanced people that control the unbalanced power. Life is tough, prickly, tricky, sticky and persistently feckin' demanding– so let's celebrate fandom and the exhilaration it brings. It's fundamental to us; it's valuable, part of our make-up and a massive part of our lives

These words sum it up beautifully;

"As I get older the adoration increases, I'm never without him. It's almost biblical, it's like carrying your rosary around with you"

Morrissey on Oscar Wilde - but it could be the MozArmy view on Morrissey.

SHOPPING TOLLEYS, SEAGULLS, SURVIVAL AND SPLASH.

This project has been so much fun and led me so kindly and sweetly to back and forth correspondence with the delightful MozArmy. I am so sorry, I couldn't place all contributions into this project. Next time, perhaps? Wonderfully worded conversations or emails have been so interesting, deep, perceptive, witty, and intelligent with sincere expressions of love for our hero Morrissey.

Morrissey and MozArmy - I do hope I've made you all proud.

Without Morrissey many emotions would be redundant. With him, we are the world's strongest emotional legion. Finding Morrissey has been the pinnacle of my life and he has brought everything I ever wanted and more.

The songs are fascinating tales and diary entries that move me at any part of the day. Morrissey wasn't just for a period of time, his work, his words are timeless. Whatever the world offers – Morrissey is there. I offer Morrissey sincere thanks for everything he has provided in the past and the present and for the future.

The feedback and stories received have been honest and open accounts from fans. When I asked for stories to be submitted, initially, I was so happy that people said 'yes'. As I am a no one and they are someone. But, they agreed and I was delighted and amazed again, as the stories were so honest and open and merged into a perfect tale of fondness and devotion. Morrissey is part of the lives of so many and always will be.

As I scribble down these final words (thank goodness for that I hear you say), I was sat on the banks of the Mersey.

It was fairly warm, but a coat and scarf was required. I was a couple of miles away from home at Otterspool promenade in South Liverpool. It was quiet but there were still families in the distance. I could hear the playful exuberance of youth as the parents asked nicely for the children to calm down and to get ready to go home for tea. Parents asked the children to stop kicking a ball and to also stop kicking each other. Joggers jogged and fishermen murdered – but vocally congratulated each other's killer technique. The fishermen not the joggers.

The sun weakened as the night drew in. I read over the tales from fans as I listened to Morrissey and The Smiths. On shuffle, I played the songs to save my life. I smiled at the tales from the community of fans. The natural progression from special times with Morrissey had become much more as the fandom and obsession took over lives and their homes. The language suggested religious questions. And language still wants them answered.

I looked across the Mersey to the areas of land I can wave to, but I've never been to. The northern streets and industrial zones in the distance made me smile. I could see as far as, well, over there. And flickering and bickering, staccato lights told me the world was alive but, everyone was at home, work and play - time over, teatime ready.

I decided to walk home and made my way down the long promenade. The grey flat path led me in the direction of home. And although I wasn't tired I stopped for a quick pit stop to look out at the view. I was content, not that happy, but I was content. I stopped and propped myself against the railing. Looking down I could see the edge of the Mersey water making its way back to slap and tickle the walls of the promenade. The murky Mersey was ready to come home to rest against the promenade walls. Just for a few hours until Mother Nature asked the waves to go out and play again.

Down below me, on the banks of the Mersey a shopping trolley was lodged, in sludge, mire and grime and a seagull sat on the handle bar of the trolley. I noticed the seagull was looking for food – not in the trolley obviously, but around the vicinity. It stood up and its inquisitive eyes patrolled the area. It's head twitching from left to right at a 100mph. It was ready for the fight for food. It was looking at everything, every noise and movement gave the bird optimism that nourishment was nearby. The excited bird had made its home and very own watch tower on the trolley located just inches away from the promenade wall, just before the water's edge.

The bird scooped and attacked anything representing food. I then noticed it take the small amount of cuisine back to what was I presume - its family. They waited for its return, all wanting food, all wanting survival. I smiled and urged the bird to find some food. I cheered as each successful claim of food and trip to its family provided substance.

I then thought how we, as humans, or as close to humans are too- scavenging for survival. And then, I knew this peace couldn't last; total disaster and sadness. BANG, BANG, SPLASH! Oh no, No, No'ooooo…..!

Peering over the railing, I had dropped all of my papers and more. My water bottle hit my foot, then bounced off my foot and made its journey under the railing to drop with force, into the Mersey below me.

I then watched as my papers scattered around me, but more importantly a picture of Morrissey floated slowly and carefully towards the seagull and the shopping trolley.

Oh to be that seagull, oh to be that shopping trolley.